MAGNA CARTA

THE MAKING AND LEGACY
OF THE GREAT CHARTER

[illegible]

… et si nos diviserimus ut viderimus eum in exercitum, erit quietus de custodia secundum quantitatem temporis quo per nos fuerit in exercitu. Nullus …

… convicti fuerint de felonia nisi per unum annum et unum diem, et tunc reddantur terre dominis feodorum. Omnes kidelli decetero deponantur penitus de Tam…

…don. et una latitudo pannorum tinctorum et russettorum et halbergettorum, scilicet due ulne infra listas. De ponderibus autem sit ut de mensuris. Nichil …

… occasione illius feodifirme vel sokagii vel burgagii, nec habebimus custodiam illius feodifirme vel sokagii vel burgagii nisi ipsa feodifirma de…

… legem suam sine testibus fidelibus ad hoc inductis. Nullus liber homo capiatur vel imprisonetur aut dissaisiatur aut utlagetur aut exuletur …

… per Angliam tam per terram quam per aquam ad emendum et vendendum sine omnibus malis toltis, per antiquas et rectas consuetudines, preterquam in tempore gwerre …

… tales sunt in terra. Liceat unicuique decetero exire de regno nostro et redire salvo et secure per terram et per aquam, salva fide nostra, nisi tempore gw…

de aliqua escaeta que sunt in manu nostra et sunt baronie, et obierit, heres eius non det aliud relevium nec faciat nobis aliud servicium quam faceret baroni …

… non faciemus justiciarios, constabularios, vicecomites vel ballivos, nisi de talibus qui sciant legem regni et eam bene velint observare. Omnes barones qui …

… consuetudines de forestis et warennis et de forestariis et warennariis, vicecomitibus et eorum ministris, ripariis et earum custodibus, statim inquirantur in …

… securitatem pacis vel fidelis servicii. Nos amovebimus penitus de balliis parentes Gerardi de Athyes quod decetero nullam habeant balliam in Anglia, Engelard…

…balistarios, servientes, stipendiarios qui veniunt cum equis et armis ad nocumentum regni. Si quis fuerit dissaisitus vel elongatus per nos sine legali iudicio pa…

… Henricum regem patrem nostrum vel per Ricardum regem fratrem nostrum, que in manu nostra habemus vel que alii tenent, que nos oporteat warantizare, respectum h…

… habebimus de forestis deafforestandis que Henricus pater noster vel Ricardus frater noster afforestaverunt, et de custodiis terrarum que sunt de alieno feodo, cuiusmodi …

Nullus capiatur nec imprisonetur propter appellum femine de morte alterius quam viri sui. Omnes fines qui iniuste et contra legem terre facti sunt nobiscum, et omnia am…

… nichilominus procedat negocium sine eo, ita quod si aliquis vel aliqui de predictis viginti quinque baronibus fuerint in simili querela, amoveantur quantum ad hoc iudici…

… inde fiat in marchia per iudicium parium suorum, de tenementis Anglie secundum legem Anglie, de tenementis Wallie secundum legem Wallie, de tenementis marchie …

… oporteat warantizare, respectum habebimus usque ad communem terminum crucesignatorum, exceptis illis de quibus placitum motum fuit vel inquisicio f…

… in securitatem pacis. Nos faciemus Alexandro regi Scottorum de sororibus suis et obsidibus reddendis, et libertatibus suis et iure suo secundum formam in qua fa…

de regno nostro, tam clerici quam laici observent quantum ad se pertinet erga suos. Cum autem pro Deo et ad emendacionem regni nostri et ad melius sopiend…

… tenere et facere observari pacem et libertates quas eis concessimus et hac presenti carta nostra confirmavimus, ita scilicet quod si nos vel justiciarius noster vel b…

… proponentes nobis excessum, petent ut excessum illum sine dilatione faciamus emendari. Et si nos excessum non emendaverimus vel si fuerimus extra …

… communa tocius terre distringent et gravabunt nos modis omnibus quibus poterunt, scilicet per capcionem castrorum, terrarum, possessionum, et aliis modis quibus poterunt, do…

… suo cum ipsis, et nos publice et libere damus licenciam iurandi cuilibet qui iurare voluerit, et nulli umquam iurare prohibebimus. Omnes autem illos de t…

… possent exequi, qui residui fuerint de predictis viginti quinque baronibus eligant alium loco ipsius pro arbitrio suo, qui simili modo erit iur…

… providerit vel preceperit, ac si omnes viginti quinque in hoc consensissent; et predicti viginti quinque iurent quod omnia antedicta fideliter observabunt, et pro toto …

… voluntates, indignaciones et rancores ortos inter nos et homines nostros, clericos et laicos, a tempore discordie, plene omnibus remisimus et condonavimus. Preterea omnes transgres…

… Dublinensis archiepiscopi et episcoporum predictorum et magistri Pandulfi super securitate ista et concessionibus prefatis. Quare volumus et firmiter preci…

… tam ex parte nostra quam ex parte baronum quod hec omnia supradicta bona fide et sine malo ingenio observabuntur. Testibus supradictis et multis aliis. D…

MAGNA CARTA

THE MAKING AND LEGACY
OF THE GREAT CHARTER

1 3 5 7 9 10 8 6 4 2

A catalogue record for this book is available
from the British Library.

ISBN [HB] 9781781858851
ISBN [E] 9 9781781858844

Designed by Isambard Thomas

Printed in Spain by Graficas Estella

HEAD OF ZEUS LTD
Clerkenwell House
45–47 Clerkenwell Green
London EC1R 0HT
www.headofzeus.com

INTRODUCTION

THE FAME OF MAGNA CARTA

Eight hundred years after it was first agreed beneath the oak trees of Runnymede, by the fertile green banks of the River Thames, Magna Carta is more famous than ever. This is strange. In its surviving forms – and there are four known original charters dating from June 1215 – Magna Carta is something of a muddle. It is a collection of promises extracted in bad faith from a reluctant king, most of which concern matters of arcane thirteenth-century legal principle. A few of these promises concern themselves with high ideals, but those are few and far between, vague and idealistic statements slipped between longer and more perplexing sentences describing the 'customary fee' that a baron ought to pay a king on the occasion of coming into an inheritance, or the protocols for dealing with debt to the Crown, or the regulation of fish-traps along the Thames and the Medway.

For the most part, Magna Carta is dry, technical, difficult to decipher and constitutionally obsolete. Those parts that are still frequently quoted – clauses about the right to justice before one's peers, the freedom from being unlawfully imprisoned and the freedom of the Church – did not mean in 1215 what we often wish they would mean today. They are part of an agreement drawn up not to defend, in perpetuity, the interests of national citizens, but rather to pin down a king who had been greatly vexing a very small number of wealthy and violent barons. Magna Carta ought to be dead, defunct and only of interest to serious scholars of the thirteenth century.

Yet it is very much alive, one of the most hallowed documents in the world, revered from the Arctic Circle to the Antipodes, written into the constitutions of numerous countries, and admired as a foundation stone in the Western traditions of liberty, democracy and the rule of law. How did that happen?

This book tells the story of Magna Carta – its background, its birth, its almost instantaneous failure, its slow resurrection and its mutation into the thing it is today: a historical palimpsest onto which almost any dream can be written. It looks at Magna Carta's place in the history of medieval England

and modern Britain. It describes briefly how the charter was exported to America and the wider world. It considers how Magna Carta is discussed in the popular media today, as we enter the ninth century of its existence. It also presents the text in its Latin form and, more accessibly, in English translation, so that readers can, as it were, go straight to the horse's mouth.

Mostly, though, this book seeks to explain the historical context from which Magna Carta emerged in the early thirteenth century, during the reign of King John. His rule was a litany of troubles, which included the loss of Normandy in 1204, a great argument with Pope Innocent III (in the course of which England's churches closed and John himself was excommunicated), vicious personal squabbles with barons whom the king had once called his friends, an utterly miserable invasion of France in 1214, and finally civil war in 1215–17, as a result of which Magna Carta was produced and John succumbed to fatal illness. I have told this story in detail, and have tried to describe how the policies John pursued built towards Magna Carta in 1215, and why his barons felt so compelled to shackle him as they did.

This book does not attempt to drastically rehabilitate John, who was satirized so deliciously in Sellar and Yeatman's *1066 and All That* as 'an awful king'. It does, however, aim to show that Magna Carta had far deeper roots than John's reign. While John's own, often appalling, behaviour was much to blame for the chaos that rained down upon him during his final years, he was not by any means the sole architect of his woes. This is a point recognized both by modern historians and by men who lived in the age of Magna Carta. The chronicler Ralph of Coggeshall, writing in the middle of the thirteenth century, observed that Magna Carta was not created simply to restrain John but also to end 'the evil customs which the father and brother of the king had created to the detriment of the Church and kingdom, along with those abuses which the king had added'.[1] Gerald of Wales, who was always inclined to anti-Plantagenet hysteria in his writing, agreed, calling John a 'tyrannous whelp,' but admitted that he had 'issued from the most bloody tyrants'.[2] This was typical Geraldic exaggeration; nevertheless, it

nods us in the direction of an important historical truth: we cannot simply view Magna Carta as a bill of protest and remedy aimed merely at the scandalous and unlucky John, but as a howl of historical complaint that was directed, at least on some level, against two generations of perceived abuse.

To begin this story, therefore, we must reach back sixty years before 1215, to the time of John's father, Henry II.

Dan Jones
Battersea, London
October 2014

1

ENGLAND REORDERED

1154–1189

King John's father, Henry II, was a man who made an impression. It is true that physically he was not much to look at: a little more than middling height, solidly built, with bowed legs and grey eyes that were said to flash when he grew angry. The force of his character, however, made him unforgettable. Henry possessed near-boundless energy. 'Perpetually wakeful and at work,' wrote the courtier and chronicler Walter Map; but this scarcely did justice to his sheer will and determination.[1] By the time Henry Plantagenet was crowned King of England on 19 December 1154, aged twenty-one, he had already laid claim to the titles of Duke of Normandy, Duke of Aquitaine – by virtue of marriage in 1152 to Eleanor of Aquitaine – and Count of Anjou.* During his reign he would take effective command of Brittany and assert his right to the lordship of Ireland. His power therefore stretched from the borders of Scotland to the Pyrenees, and they encompassed virtually the entire western seaboard of greater France. Indeed, Henry's political tentacles stretched even further afield than that, for he had interests and alliances from Saxony to Sicily, and from Castile to the Holy Land. Few European monarchs since Charlemagne had exercised control over such vast territories, and few medieval kings would rule with such political agility, ruthlessness and skill.

Henry's physical stamina allowed him to spend almost his whole life moving about his lands, 'tolerant of the discomforts of dust and mud ... travelling in unbearably long stages', and enjoying, according to Walter Map, the fact that his physical exertions prevented him from getting fat.[2] He astonished his rival rulers with the ability to pop up where they least expected him, and he both charmed and scared those who worked for him, by dint of his tendency to slip in an instant from bluff good humour to foaming rage. During one infamous tantrum, Henry thrashed about on the floor of his

---

*   It was by virtue of possession of the County of Anjou that the continental holdings of Henry II and his sons Richard I and John are sometimes referred to as the Angevin Empire.

chamber, gnawing at the straw from his mattress. But it was Henry's born talent for politics and government that most struck those who met him. Writing after the king's death, the Yorkshire chronicler William of Newburgh opined that the king 'seemed to possess notable wisdom, stability, and a passion for justice,' and that even from 'his earliest days' Henry 'conveyed the impression of a great ruler'.[3]

Henry inherited the English crown in a political deal to end a civil war that had raged for nineteen years. Contemporaries called the war the 'Shipwreck'. Historians now refer to it as the 'Anarchy'. Either way, it was a struggle waged between two grandchildren of William the Conqueror – Henry's mother, Matilda, and her cousin, King Stephen, both of whom claimed to be the legitimate heir of Henry I (r. 1100–35).*

Neither contender for the throne could summon enough military or political support to enforce their claim, and as a result England was torn for a generation between two hostile factions. Royal authority across the realm collapsed, and the horrors of civil war descended: arson, torture, bloodshed, murder, robbery, laying waste the land, starvation, economic turmoil and a widespread failure of justice. 'Every man began to rob his neighbour,' wrote the author of the Anglo-Saxon Chronicle. 'It was said openly that Christ and his saints were asleep.'[4] The Treaty of Winchester (1153) brought an end to the conflict by naming Henry as Stephen's royal heir. When Stephen died the following year and Henry took power, his first duty was to restore firm royal rule to a land that had not known effective governance for a generation.

There were three basic, determining conditions to Henry II's rule in England. The first was his urgent need to impose order after the Anarchy. The second was his need to create a political system that would allow him to

---

*   Matilda was Henry I's only legitimate daughter, and she used the title 'Empress' following her marriage to Henry V, King of Germany and Holy Roman Emperor (d.1125). Stephen's mother was Henry I's sister Adela of Blois. Stephen and Matilda were therefore first cousins.

Henricus natus matildis regna tenebat.
Sub quo sanctus thomas mucrone cadebat

Henricus secundus genuit.

rule his kingdom efficiently while he travelled across the rest of his territories fighting his enemies, chief among them being Louis VII, King of France. The third was a constant need to raise money. Henry approached these problems with a natural instinct for strong, centralized government and a knack for financially squeezing his subjects – particularly those in England, the richest part of his empire. In doing so, he put his personal stamp on the style and substance of all royal government in a way that would come to define the sixty years before Magna Carta.

Henry loved control. Although in England, as in the rest of his lands, he was happy to delegate the business of government to trusted advisers, he made it very clear from the beginning that power stemmed ultimately – and only – from the king. At his coronation he imitated his Norman predecessors by issuing a charter that promised to protect 'all the concessions and grants and liberties and free customs' granted to the Church and the great men of the kingdom by Henry I, and likewise to abolish all the 'evil customs' that had sprung up in the realm. But this was the last such concession that he would make. Although Henry II made a great effort to rally to his side as many of the great men of England as he could, he was also prepared to break the power of the handful of English barons who dared to defy him, while leaving the rest in no doubt to whom they owed their positions of wealth and prestige. He razed castles that had been built during the civil war and expelled foreign mercenaries. He reissued the coinage and imposed heavy penalties on those who forged or clipped his coins.* He cancelled all grants of land and office that had been made under Stephen; those he saw fit to re-grant were given back explicitly under his own authority. He refused to relinquish command of any territory or property where it might result in his

---

* Regulating and stabilizing the money supply was both a mark of kingly authority and a means of combatting financial fraud. Coin clipping was seen as an especially pernicious activity: by shaving off the edges of coins, clippers could harvest the silver and mint their own, fake, coins.

own power being diminished, and he took great pains to punish anyone who opposed him. And most importantly for the long-term history of England, Henry oversaw a legal and administrative revolution that allowed his authority to be felt in the realm even when he was absent – as he would be for around two-thirds of his thirty-five-year reign.

'Wealth is obviously necessary not only in wartime but also in peacetime,' wrote Richard FitzNigel, royal treasurer and Bishop of London, in a practical guidebook to royal finance known as 'The Dialogue of the Exchequer'. FitzNigel (also known as FitzNeal) completed his book in the late 1180s, around the time that Henry II died, and his words reflect a lifetime in service to a king whose need for money was always pressing. Under Henry's rule, the Exchequer became the most important institution of royal government, for it was there that royal revenues were accounted, on a large table, ten feet by five feet, which was covered with a cloth resembling a chessboard, and it was through the Exchequer that the king could levy heavy financial penalties on those subjects who displeased him. It received fines imposed by the king's judges and it handled bribes paid by landholders who sought royal favour in disputes with their neighbours. Feudal dues – customary payments made by aristocrats for the king's permission to marry or inherit – came across the chequered cloth-covered table, and so did taxes such as 'scutage', also known as 'shield-money', a payment made by barons to avoid sending their loyal knights to fight in royal armies (and which, in theory, might then be used to buy mercenaries).[*]

During the civil war, the Exchequer had lost its teeth: sheriffs – key royal officials in the shires of England – had stopped rendering their accounts before it, and the barons of England had avoided paying their feudal

---

[*] 'Feudalism' has been a much-debated term, but its essence in this period is a hierarchical ordering of society in which a system of obligations (notably military, but also financial) existed in return for the possession of land, property and other rights. At the top of the hierarchy was, of course, the Crown, from which leading men held land as 'tenants-in-chief'.

dues. But this decline was dramatically reversed under Henry. FitzNigel's handbook shows us just what a wide array of business came before Henry's Exchequer. Its officials counted and sorted silver coins, audited sheriffs' accounts for revenues raised in the shires, received scutage and fines paid by communities for murders committed (where there was no culprit discovered), as well as taking in fines paid for abuses committed in royal forest land. They took receipt of falcons and hawks given as gifts to the king and they handled 'queen's gold' – a tax of 1 mark of gold for every 100 marks of silver owed to the king.*

The Exchequer was a huge and complex government department. Yet it is clear that Henry regarded it as not only a financial institution, but also as a political tool. The Marshal of the Exchequer had the power to arrest those who came before it insolvent. Powerful subjects could be ruined without taking up arms against them, simply by calling in large debts they owed to the Crown. Equally, the king could reward men who were in his favour by reducing, rescheduling or cancelling their debts. Very few barons paid everything they owed the Exchequer. Indeed, some of the king's close associates – such as Robert, Earl of Leicester and Reginald, Earl of Cornwall – paid nothing at all on their debts.[5] Despite these selective exemptions, however, Henry's general insistence on tight financial governance bore fruit. Early in his reign, about £13,000 a year crossed the Exchequer table. By the 1180s the flow of money stood at £22,000 – testament not only to rising revenue, necessary to help the king defend his vast lands, but also to a king exerting a much tighter royal grip, even *in absentia*, on the great men of his realm.[6]

Having reformed royal finance, Henry set about changing the way that royal justice worked. Starting in 1163–6, sweeping reforms affected

---

* A mark – which was a unit of calculation rather than physical coinage – was held to be worth 13 shillings and 4 pence, and therefore two-thirds of £1.

the way that the king's subjects interacted with royal law.* The Assize of Clarendon – a legal Act of 1166 – commanded that all crimes in England were to be investigated by the Crown, regardless of any local jurisdictions held by the great lords of the realm. The investigating was done not by potentially corruptible sheriffs and local officials, but by a high-powered commission of royal judges who travelled on a circuit known as the General Eyre, and who investigated cases with juries of twelve local men rather than committing defendants to judgment by ordeal of fire or by 'compurgation', as had been the case in the past.† Most importantly the assize meant that all murder, robbery and theft now came under royal jurisdiction; ten years later the Assize of Northampton added arson, forgery and counterfeiting to this list.

It was not only the scope of criminal law that expanded under Henry. There was also a revolution in the way that civil law in England operated. Land disputes were the source of a huge volume of litigation during the Middle Ages, and Henry made the process by which the Crown could intervene in cases smoother, easier and more profitable. Since before the Norman Conquest it had been possible to apply for royal justice by seeking a 'writ' from the government department known as Chancery. A writ was a short chit, which could initiate legal action in royal courts or command a royal sheriff to carry out some form of action to remedy a wrong. These were generally *ad hoc*, non-standard official devices. Henry made a series of standardized writs available, most importantly the writs of 'novel disseizin', 'mort

---

* The chief point to remember regarding lawmaking at this time is that it was the era before Parliament and before statutes; laws were made by kings and their counsellors; other laws and customs existed at local levels, while the Church stiffly maintained its aloofness from secular laws, seeing its own ecclesiastical law as answerable to the pope – a cause of tensions that exploded in Henry II's conflict with Thomas Becket.

† Under the system of compurgation, a defendant who could find sufficient neighbours to swear to his innocence would walk free. The Assize of Clarendon abolished this.

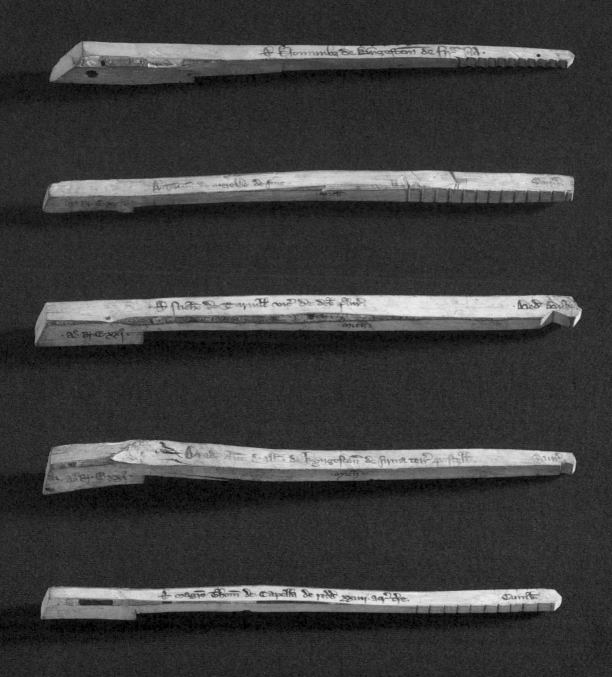

d'ancestor' and the writ of right: respectively these protected landholders from having their land illegally seized by lords or third parties, asserted the right to inherit land, and instructed a sheriff to 'do right' by the holder of the writ. They were simple, formulaic and straightforward to obtain, whether or not the king was in the country. The reach of the Crown thus began to extend deep down into English society, as the royal law became more available, desirable and widely used than ever before. Moreover, writs cost money, and their increasing popularity brought the Crown a handsome profit from litigants' fees and fines. Best of all, none of this required Henry's personal presence. A money-making bureaucratic machine was born.

Not everyone, however, was happy, and just as we can trace to Henry II's reign the origins of the royal system against which Magna Carta was aimed, so we can trace the first rumblings of dissatisfaction and protest to which Magna Carta responded.

In 1163, Henry attempted to browbeat his erstwhile friend, servant and boon companion Thomas Becket, whom he had appointed Archbishop of Canterbury, into allowing the Crown to place on trial and punish 'criminous clerks' – churchmen who had committed crimes. This was an age that still possessed a separate system of church law, and these proposals would have been a huge invasion of secular law into ecclesiastical jurisdiction. Becket's refusal to allow it prompted the famous breach between the two men, which ended with the archbishop's heinous murder before the altar of Canterbury Cathedral in 1170. His quarrel with Henry stemmed from a fundamental, unbridgable divergence: the archbishop viewed the king as a tyrant, who was riding roughshod over the law, while Henry saw only that he was exercising his royal prerogatives. When Becket went into exile from England, between 1164 and 1170, he wrote a series of angry and insulting letters to, and about, the king, including one to Henry's mother Matilda, in which he complained that '[Henry] is afflicting the churches of his realm beyond endurance and demanding from them unheard-of and unaccustomed things'. Cruel blows and bitter insults were being traded between English kings and the English

OPPOSITE
A collection of tally sticks, which were used in accounting in the medieval English Exchequer. Each stick was split between the Exchequer and the other party, and the notches in both parts were supposed to align, showing the status of loans and payments. The king's Exchequer could ruin barons in a single day by calling in all the debts that were owed to the Crown, and John's exploitation of this power would earn him the hatred of many of his subjects. (In 1834, the fire that burnt down the Houses of Parliament began as a controlled bonfire of old tally sticks.)

Church long before King John's reign. This tension would come to underpin much of what emerged in Magna Carta.

As much as anything else, Henry II set the tone for early Plantagenet kingship – or so it would appear from the comfortable distance of his youngest son's reign. He set out a platform of aggressive, disciplined, rigorous kingship that was highly adept at milking cash from England and channelling it to the continent. He pushed the financial and judicial power of the Crown deep into the shires. He oversaw a dramatic reduction of the military power of the major barons, for as well as razing baronial castles following the Anarchy, Henry seized huge numbers of them following the rebellion known as the 'Great War' in 1173–4. In 1154 the Crown held something like 35 per cent of England's 350 castles; by the 1180s that figure had risen substantially, and by John's reign nearly half of England's castles were in royal hands.[7]

Henry also occasionally lived up to his ancestors' reputations for diabolical cruelty. Old family legend had it that the Angevins were descended from the devil, and there were Englishmen who saw something demonic in the character of the king. Writers hostile to Henry, such as Ralph Niger, accused him not only of demeaning the nobility of his greatest subjects, but also of being an irreligious tyrant and a slavering womanizer. Even William of Newburgh, who generally wrote kindly of Henry, recorded that in his day 'he was hateful to nearly everyone'.[8] This may have been an exaggeration, but Henry was certainly capable of a ferocity that tested the limits even of a violent age. His worst malice was shown in his treatment of Becket's followers, hundreds of whom were stripped of their possessions, sent into exile or imprisoned in chains during Henry's quarrel with the archbishop. Clerics who attempted to proclaim the religious penalties imposed by Becket on the king could have their eyes put out, or feet or genitals hacked off in punishment. Even messengers were not safe: a young boy who passed the king vexing letters from the pope was tortured by having his eyes gouged and being forced to drink boiling water.[9] And of course, the archbishop himself was cut down,

if not on Henry's orders then at least at his unwitting instigation. These deeds would not be forgotten by the generation that followed; indeed, the murderous cruelty of the old king seemed to be the prelude to the even worse behaviour of his sons.

Henry II died at the Plantagenet fortress of Chinon, in the Loire, during the hot summer of 1189. His later years had been made miserable by struggles with a new French king, Philip II 'Augustus', and wars with his impatient and rebellious children over their inheritances. His eldest adult son with Eleanor, Henry 'the Young King', predeceased him (as did their third son, Geoffrey), and so it was Richard 'the Lionheart' who was crowned King of England at Westminster Abbey on Sunday 3 September 1189. Richard would become one of the most celebrated kings in British history; he remains the only monarch to be commemorated with a statue outside the Houses of Parliament. This is ironic, for of all the kings who reigned after the Norman Conquest, Richard probably spent the least time – and took the least personal interest – in his English kingdom. His reign would see his father's reforms and policies pushed to greater extremes. It would also see the arrival on the political stage of Richard's controversial and deeply untrustworthy youngest brother, John 'Lackland', the man who would come to suffer the consequences of all his family's misdeeds.

2

WAR AND TAXES

1189–1199

Richard I's heart, leonine as it was, never truly lay in England. Today it can be found in Normandy, at Rouen Cathedral, where the mummified remains of the organ (removed from his body at death) have collapsed into a pile of greyish-brown powder, mingled together with grains of frankincense, daisy, mint and myrtle, the substances that were used to preserve it. But in the prime of Richard's life, this heart throbbed with a lust for warfare and adventure, which was fulfilled on battlefields from western France to the plains of the Holy Land.

Although Richard was born in Oxford, his mother, Eleanor of Aquitaine, raised him as a prince of the wild French South. He subsequently spent most of his adult life outside England and tended to return only when he was truly desperate for money. Nevertheless, the absent Lionheart's grand military ambition would have a profound effect on the realm that gave him his crown, and this most un-English of kings would have his own part to play in the history of that most English of documents, Magna Carta.

Like many of the boldest young men of the age, Richard I was a crusader. He was crowned less than a week before his thirty-second birthday, by which time he had already taken the cross and promised solemnly to make his armed pilgrimage to 'Outremer', as the Christian lands in the Middle East were then known. The Third Crusade had been called as a response to the fall of Acre and Jerusalem to forces under the great Muslim sultan Saladin. It galvanized princes across Europe, including the French king, Philip Augustus, and the Holy Roman Emperor, Frederick Barbarossa. The King of England had no intention of being left behind.

'The son, becoming greater and greater, enlarged the good works of his father, while the bad ones he cut short.' Such was chronicler Roger of Howden's initial assessment of Richard's succession to the English crown.[1] But it is largely a piece of flattery from a writer who had close connections at court and who travelled extensively with his king about the Holy Land. It is true that Richard, like Henry II, promised at his coronation to protect the liberties of the English Church and to provide justice to his subjects.

However, as Howden reports in a more truthful phrase, once the king was crowned and had taken oaths of allegiance from all his nobles, he 'put up for sale everything he had'.[2] Crusading was a dazzlingly expensive business, and Richard drained his new realm for everything it had. As hired ships were loaded with thousands of salted pig carcasses, horseshoes, arrows and other provisions necessary to fight a long war far from home, so the king's leading subjects were exploited by every means available. Castles, offices, lands and lordships were effectively auctioned off to them in a frenzy of selling before the king set sail. Henry II had designed a slick system of government that could raise money efficiently and operate in the king's absence. Richard drove the machine with single-minded vigour.

The pipe rolls of Richard's reign point to 1190 as a year of impressive financial exaction.* A special tax known as the Saladin Tithe had been levied across the Plantagenet Empire to help pay for the costs of crusading. This was supplemented with a year of intense royal fundraising through the regular channels of government. Whereas £22,000 was the regular royal income shown on the pipe rolls of Henry II's later years, in 1190 Richard managed to extract £31,089 from his realm – a jump of close to 50 per cent.[3] The bulk of this rise came from two sources – the profits of justice and the exploitation of Richard's feudal rights as king. The former included fees charged for access to royal courts via writs, the sale of official positions (including most of England's shrievalties – the office of sheriff) and the confirmation of charters that had been previously granted by Henry II. On top of this, the king imposed heavy feudal levies on his barons in the form of payments they had to make for permission to marry, to inherit or to exercise wardship over under-age heirs. The crusade inflation on these

---

* Pipe rolls were the annual records of royal finances, kept by the Exchequer, and so called because the long documents (of parchment, made from sheepskin) were rolled up to form pipe-shapes. An almost complete run of these records exist from the mid-12th century to the early nineteenth century.

WAR AND TAXES

payments was sharp, and it must have been with some relief, as well as excitement, that England bade farewell to its energetic and zealous new ruler when he left Dover in December 1189, two months after his coronation, on his heroic quest to destroy the Infidel armies who were polluting Jerusalem with their unholy presence. He would be gone for more than four years.

Richard's reputation in his day (and ever since) was founded on his peerless brilliance as a military leader. He had a good crusade, fighting his way through Sicily, conquering Cyprus and arriving in splendour in Outremer, just in time to participate in the last stages of the successful siege of Acre. Once the city fell, Richard reinforced Jaffa and Ascalon (Ashkelon today, in Israel) and secured a three-year truce with Saladin, during which time unarmed Christian pilgrims were granted safe access to Jerusalem. By the time he left the Holy Land in October 1192, Richard was famous across the known world and had made himself the object of admiration by Saladin. Unfortunately, he had also made some powerful enemies among his Christian allies, and on his way back to Europe Richard was shipwrecked off the north-east Italian coast, captured by Duke Leopold of Austria and sold to the Holy Roman Emperor, Henry VI, who jailed him at Trifels Castle, high in the mountains of what is now south-western Germany. The price of his freedom was a vast ransom of 150,000 marks (£100,000) – roughly the price of another crusade – which had to be raised in a matter of months. For the second time in less than five years, England was bled to pay for the adventures of its charismatic ruler.

That England paid Richard's ransom at all was down to the efforts of the level-headed and loyal men whom the king had placed in charge of England's government during his absence. They included William Longchamp, Bishop of Ely; Walter of Coutances, Bishop of Rouen; and Hubert Walter, Archbishop of Canterbury. They were directed by the king's 'much-beloved' mother, Eleanor, now in her late sixties but still a regal force of nature.[4] Together, they worked Europe's diplomatic channels, found hostages and ships when these were demanded by the king's captors, levied a

WAR AND TAXES

25 per-cent tax on income and movables, requisitioned a whole year's supply of wool from England's Cistercian abbeys, and followed up Richard's personal request for English churches to send 'the whole of the gold and silver' that they kept, which he promised to return on his release.[5] Astonishingly, 100,000 marks – two-thirds of the ransom – was raised within a year, and on 4 February 1194 Richard was released, quite literally into the arms of his mother. He returned to England on 13 March, wore his crown in a ceremony at Westminster Abbey a month later and went on a rapid tour of his kingdom. Then, on 12 May 1194, he put to sea at Portsmouth, leaving to defend Normandy and the rest of his continental possessions from attack by King Philip Augustus. Another round of expensive military campaigning loomed. As it turned out, Richard would have five years' more fighting ahead of him. As it also turned out, he would never see his kingdom again.

Between 1194 and 1199 Richard performed some mighty military deeds. During his crusade and captivity, his continental lands had been sorely depleted, mainly thanks to the efforts of his feckless brother John. Although John had been bribed to stay out of England during the king's absence – being granted a massive income from the revenues of six English counties and the Royal Duchy of Lancaster, as well as the continental title of 'Count of Mortain' – he had ignored orders, entering the country and provoking armed confrontations with Richard's officials, and trying to seize control of government for himself. Then, when his English machinations had faltered, John had gone over to the continent, where he allied himself with the French king and agreed to grant away Richard's most strategically important lands and mighty castles in return for Philip Augustus recognizing him as rightful ruler of Plantagenet holdings in France. Magnanimously, if not wisely, Richard forgave John almost immediately on his release in 1194 – and then set about his war with France. The result was a long and bloody series of campaigns, merely to restore his lands to their condition and extent as inherited from Henry II.

Richard's sphere of operations stretched from the Vexin, a hotly disputed portion of land on the border between Normandy and the lands directly controlled by Philip Augustus, to Brittany, Berry, Poitou and Limoges. Costly alliances were made with men like Richard's former captor, Emperor Henry VI, as well as Baldwin, Count of Flanders, and a large number of other noblemen whose borders touched France. An extraordinary military supply chain was set up, connecting Portsmouth with the Norman castle-towns along the Seine, culminating in a magnificent fortified palace at Les Andelys, known as Château Gaillard, which was built at massive expense (at least £12,000, or half a year's English royal income) in just two years, between 1196 and 1198. The war was fought on land and from the sea, and it provided men like William Marshal, one of the most famous knights of the age, with a wealth of anecdotes and tall-tales to tell their grandchildren.[6] And it was supremely successful. By January 1199 Richard's enemies had been beaten into submission on every front and he was planning seriously to go east once again for the Fourth Crusade proposed by a new pope, Innocent III.

Another look at Richard's accounts shows us that England paid handsomely for this long process of restoration and reconquest. Analysis of the pipe rolls has shown that during the period 1194–8 the average revenue taken from England was nearly £25,000, peaking in 1196 when £28,323 went through the books.[7] Once again, the processes of justice, the king's feudal rights and taxation (such as scutage) were exploited to scoop money out of England for use across the Channel. And there were innovations, too. In 1198 the king levied a 'carucage' – a new land tax, initially assessed according to the size of estates as recorded in Domesday Book.* This raised £1,000 and appears to have been unpopular, since Richard's officials were obliged to investigate and punish with fines numerous instances of avoidance. In the short term such measures brought Richard the means with which to cow Europe with his

---

* A 'carucate' was the amount of land that could be ploughed by an eight-ox team in a year: somewhere between 100 and 120 acres.

untouchable military brilliance. In the long term, however, problems were starting to build, which would surface years later with Magna Carta.

Richard's death came suddenly, and shockingly, in the spring of 1199. While commanding a siege at the castle of Châlus-Chabrol in the Limousin on 26 March, he was hit in the shoulder by a speculative crossbow bolt fired from a battlement by a man using a frying-pan for a shield. The wound was attended to by a field surgeon but went gangrenous, and by 11 April the Lionheart was dead.

Despite a marriage to Berengaria of Navarre, Richard had never had any children. He left his empire intact, his crown somewhat impoverished – and his brother John as his heir. It was a combination that would have disastrous consequences.

3

EMPIRE'S END

1199–1204

People loathed John. For all the attempts that have been made by historians to rehabilitate his reputation, any study of England's third Plantagenet ruler must account for the fact that he was a cruel and unpleasant man, a second-rate soldier and a slippery, faithless, interfering king. It is true that at times John was no *less* ruthless than his brother Richard, nor any less manipulative than his father, Henry. But if his relatives shared some of his worst traits, he shared almost none of their best.

John was, it must be admitted, an excellent administrator, who knew his way around the departments of his own government, took an expert personal interest in the workings of royal justice and kept a lavish, open-handed court. But these were not the primary measures by which men of his time assessed him, and even if we allow for the fact that some of the best surviving descriptions of John were written with hindsight, by men who judged his whole life by the ignominy of its end, it is still clear that this was not a man who was considered fit for kingship.

Ralph of Coggeshall lived through John's reign and despaired of the king, pointing out his cruelty, his small-minded viciousness, his threatening manner and his childish habits of ridiculing his subjects and laughing at their misfortunes. Ralph wrote from the distance of the 1220s, once John was dead and Magna Carta had been both agreed and reissued several times. But other, more strictly contemporary, authors agreed with him. The writer known as 'The Anonymous of Béthune' thought John was wicked, petty and lecherous, and he made frequent references to John's lack of chivalry.[1] The southern French poet Bertrand de Born the Younger wrote that 'no man may ever trust him / For his heart is soft and cowardly.'[2] William of Newburgh, disgusted by John's treachery during Richard's imprisonment, called him 'nature's enemy': a man who heaped 'infinite curses on his own perfidious head'.[3] Nor was it just writers in their monasteries who despaired, although many were naturally inclined against an irreligious king who spent part of his reign unrepentantly excommunicated from the Church. John's reputation went before him. And it was a major factor in the history of his reign.

lene lerm...

tande spielo ba
liste apd chaluz
pedin it ant ec
dii regnauar
iteptnt apud
fonte ebraudi
sepult qui euit.

Henric
secund
Rey que

Ricardus Rex
sertus an
an an

Iohanes
Rex sep
timus

Henricus III.
Rex octant
an an

ne Iohannes fundauit abbaziam apd widell.lll ne huricus iii. ultra remue regnant in pace anglia gubn

By the time John came to the throne, in April 1199, he had already worked up quite a record for duplicity and troublemaking. Sent to Ireland in 1185 as a nineteen-year-old prince, he had offended the local lords as soon as he landed. Gerald of Wales, who accompanied John on the expedition, recalled that he treated the natives 'with contempt and derision, [and] even rudely pulled them by their beards, which the Irishmen wore full and long, according to the custom of their country'.[4] Later, John abandoned his dying father during the last war of Henry II's reign, in 1189. He then betrayed Richard by his stirring up of armed disputes in England, during the Third Crusade. Not only did John attempt to sell the family's lands to the King of France, but when it was apparent that Richard was going to be released from his Austrian captivity, he joined with Philip Augustus in offering to pay the Holy Roman Emperor to keep Richard locked up for longer than the agreed term. Subsequently, five years of muted loyalty to Richard, between 1194 and 1199, did very little to turn popular opinion John's way; and when the news of Richard's death spread across the Plantagenet lands, there were large numbers of people who objected very strongly to the announcement that his brother had been named as successor.

It was, in fact, only with some difficulty that John secured his succession at all. His former dealings with Philip Augustus had been craven enough to convince the French king that John was a man who could be dominated, by aggression. (As Richard put it, John was not a man who could conquer a realm by force if there was force to oppose him.[5]) Philip's judgement was correct. As soon as Richard's death was known, the French invaded the Duchy of Normandy and Philip Augustus encouraged his allies up and down the rest of the Plantagenet dominions to rise up in rebellion. As a result, John began his reign fighting a defensive war on several fronts, and in 1200 he was forced to accept the Treaty of Le Goulet, by which he did homage to the French king and acknowledged the loss of a considerable chunk of his lands in Normandy and claims to overlordship elsewhere. The chronicler Gervase of Canterbury, commenting on John's willingness to accept the less

than favourable terms of Le Goulet, wrote that he 'would rather achieve peace by negotiation than fight for his own terms, and because of this his enemies and detractors call him John Softsword'.[6]

As well as his problems with Philip, John was also troubled by the existence of a rival candidate for his lands and titles: Arthur, Duke of Brittany, son of John's late elder brother Geoffrey. Born in 1187, Arthur had just turned twelve when Richard died. But his claim to the Plantagenet crown was considered by some, including the King of France, to be superior to John's. Indeed, in 1190, Richard I had actually named Arthur – then less than three years old – as his successor should he die on crusade. Arthur and John were therefore direct rivals, a fact gleefully exploited by Philip Augustus. For the next three years – and indeed, for quite some time beyond – Arthur of Brittany would be a thorn in John's side.

John had been crowned king at Westminster Abbey on 27 May 1199; but, in the manner typical of his brother, he made it a very brief visit to England. His preoccupation even after the Treaty of Le Goulet was with defending his lands from further incursions by Philip and Arthur. This required his near-constant presence on the continent. It looked very much as though England was going to experience a third successive absentee king with a chronic need for financial support. In that sense at least, it was business as usual.

Soon, however, everything would change. In August 1200 John, having secured an annulment of his first marriage to Isabel of Gloucester, took as his wife a young girl from Aquitaine called Isabella of Angoulême. That she was twelve years old was no great outrage by the standards of the day. That she was already betrothed to someone else was more problematic. Isabella's intended was Hugh de Lusignan, and the marriage was due to draw together the two most prominent, troublesome and mutually hostile families of the Gascon South. By effectively kidnapping Hugh's bride, John achieved the impressive feat of pushing these enemy clans into each others' arms and giving Philip Augustus an excuse, in 1202, to launch a fresh round of punitive invasions of Plantagenet territories.

During the subsequent war, John managed to capture Arthur, during an impressive military operation at Mirebeau, in Anjou. But this was a rare success. John consistently antagonized and alienated his own allies, many of whom abandoned or turned on him. Within a year, Anjou, Maine, Touraine and parts of Poitou had all fallen to Philip, ripping the heart out of the Plantagenet Empire. John retreated to Normandy, taking Arthur with him. Just before Easter in 1203 Arthur disappeared, almost certainly murdered at Rouen, possibly by a drunk and angry John himself – he was said to have crushed the sixteen-year-old's head with a heavy stone and thrown his body into the River Seine. But there was little time for John to enjoy his victory.

In the summer of 1203, Philip invaded western Normandy and laid siege to Château Gaillard, the greatest symbol of Richard the Lionheart's muscular kingship. With Normandy falling around his ears, John was said to have gone into a paranoid decline, fearful to ride the open highways in case of attack and convinced that traitors lay all around him. Gossips said that he spent all day lying in bed with his young bride, Isabella. Whether or not this was true, in December 1203 John abandoned his duchy, sailing for England and leaving Normandy to its fate.

By the following summer, the supposedly impregnable Château Gaillard had fallen, and Caen, Rouen and – further south – Poitiers had all surrendered. On 31 March 1204 John's spirited but ancient mother, Eleanor of Aquitaine, died, aged eighty-two. Her formidable presence had kept some order in the empire's south, but her death prompted the King of Castile to invade Gascony. Together, all this amounted to a sudden and catastrophic collapse. Within five years of John's accession to the throne, he had lost virtually the whole continental empire that was so painstakingly assembled and defended by his father and brother. All that remained loyal was a coastal strip of Aquitaine, around Bordeaux. And this had very pronounced long-term implications for John. For the first time in more than half-a-century, a Plantagenet King of England would be obliged to live among the English people.

OVERLEAF
Detail of a thirteenth-century fresco from the chapel of St Radegund, close to the fortress of Chinon, in the Loire. It has been identified as depicting Eleanor of Aquitaine (looking backwards), John's supportive and powerful mother; and Isabella of Angoulême, John's young second wife, in whose amorous embraces he was said to have languished while his Duchy of Normandy fell to the French in 1203.

4

THE KING IN HIS KINGDOM

1204–1205

The loss of Normandy is often described, rightly, as one of the great turning points in England's medieval history. It was obviously a terrible military defeat for John, an illustration of his low stock as a leader and a blow to his reputation. There were also financial implications. The wealth – and thus the military power – of the King of France, Philip Augustus, had been growing steadily since the 1190s, boosted by territorial acquisitions including the rich Flemish County of Artois and the Vermandois. By sucking Normandy, Anjou, Maine and Touraine back into the orbit of the French Crown, Philip's position grew even stronger. Under Henry II and during Richard's early years the Plantagenet Crown had been much richer than the French Capetian royal house. Now those roles were decisively reversed.

Defeat in and ejection from Normandy therefore re-drew the political and conceptual map of Western Europe. English kings had been dukes of Normandy since William the Conqueror had stood victorious at the Battle of Hastings in 1066, and during those 148 years the two territories had become tightly bound together. Many barons loyal to the English king held lands from him on both sides of the Channel. Trade, commerce, warfare and society operated on the assumption that the realms were linked by a common ruler. There was a common Anglo-Norman aristocratic language and culture. Wrenching apart the kingdom and duchy would have profound consequences for the men and women for whom this duality was the normal order of life.

As Philip Augustus rode imperiously about Normandy, landholders were forced to come to a decision. Feudal practice did not permit a man to do homage to two vying lords, since one of the conditions of submitting to a king was to promise to serve him in war. In 1204, therefore, men with lands in England and Normandy had to make a choice – either to lay their allegiance at the feet of the English king, or to submit to France. Those who sided with John kept their English estates, but were liable to lose the land they held across the Channel. Those who decided to safeguard their Norman

property were almost instantly cut off in England. Whenever John learned that one of his lords had decided to throw in his lot with Philip Augustus, he immediately ordered his English lands to be seized by the Crown and his name to be entered onto a register known as the *Rotulus de valore terrarum Normannorum* ('Roll of the Values of the Lands of the Normans').[1] Some baronial families – including those of the famous knight and king's friend William Marshal – attempted to work around feudal protocol and hold onto some or all of their lands across the new divide, but with limited success. Only a tiny minority could make such arrangements work. It may be an exaggeration to say that the loss of Normandy drove a permanent cultural wedge between two peoples divided by the Channel, for it was not until the fourteenth century and the Hundred Years War that the English and French

England, Scotland and Wales, as drawn in the 1250s by the chronicler Matthew Paris. Hadrian's Wall indicates the notional boundary of England and Scotland. The disintegration of the continental Plantagenet Empire in 1203–4 meant that John 'Lackland' had little option but to focus attention on his English kingdom. On the British mainland, in contrast with his feebleness abroad, he was determined and ruthless in enforcing his will and overawing the Welsh and Scots.

began to regard one another as enemies and opposites. Nevertheless, the year 1204 demanded a clear choice from the Anglo-Norman nobility. Were they English subjects or not? And if so, what did that imply? The idea that England was a 'community' with collective rights would underpin much of the philosophy of Magna Carta in 1215; it was a feeling that was accelerated by the loss of Normandy in 1204.

In King John's own eyes, the loss of Normandy demanded revenge. He was acutely aware of what had been lost over 1203–4, and he was tormented by the sense that he had to win back the homeland and heartlands of his ancestors. For the next ten years John would do everything within his power to amass enough treasure, troops and foreign allies to return to the continent and reconquer what he had lost. But this was now a doubly difficult business. Without control in Normandy John lacked both a beachhead in northern France, from which to advance his armies, and a supply chain of fortresses along the Seine. He had also lost the duchy's revenues. Normandy had paid for some portion of its own defence during the reigns of Henry and Richard, but now any expedition would have to be financed in full from England. So the task was enormous. Yet John was not daunted by it. Unfortunately, this single-minded obsession would lead him into a fateful trial of strength with his own barons, the consequence of which was Magna Carta.

*

In the years that followed 1204, England got to know its new king. Whereas John's father and brother had spent very little time in their kingdom, now there was nowhere else for the monarch to go. For the first five years of John's reign he would have been known to many of his royal subjects only from his coins, from which a wrathful cartoon face glared out, eyes popping from the thin features, with flowing locks of hair and a short beard. Now, though, John made his presence strongly felt.

OPPOSITE
Detail from Matthew Paris's
map of Britain. Over 250 cities,
towns and topographical
features are named in the map.
Here, London's significance
is suggested by its relatively
elaborate, crenellated fortress
above its name, while further
upstream on the Thames is
Windsor where, close by, the
terms of Magna Carta would
be thrashed out.

Like his father, John was an irrepressibly energetic traveller. He spent his whole life on the road, his court snaking out behind him in a caravan train that was driven along at an unholy pace of up to thirty miles a day. The court never stayed in one place for more than a month, and only rarely lodged anywhere for longer than a night or two. Even before the loss of Normandy, John had shown himself inclined to visit the forgotten corners of his realm, including towns of the North like York and Newcastle, where people had previously only clapped eyes on a Plantagenet king once in a generation.[2] But this was no mere tourism. John's determination to tramp even the chilliest highways of his kingdom sprang from a deep desire to see that his government was as efficient, as wide-reaching and as profitable as possible.

Despite all the demands that had been placed on England during the earlier Plantagenet years, John's realm was rich – and getting richer. Several years of acute inflation around the turn of the century wobbled, but did not seriously damage, a rapidly diversifying economy, which one recent historian has described as experiencing 'an exceptional period of overall expansion … fuelled to a great extent by a tremendous surge in commercial activity'.[3] New towns, markets and fairs were being founded at a record rate. Goods were being transported faster and further, as England's farmers switched to horses (rather than oxen) to pull carts which were often clad in iron around the rim to prevent them from shattering on long journeys along potholed roads. An international trade in wool and cloth was beginning to boom, bringing great quantities of produce and coin in and out of the ports of the South-East.[4] This was a realm from which a king fixated on fighting an expensive war of reconquest could quite reasonably decide to take his cut.

John took to his task with gusto. His methods stayed true to those of his Plantagenet predecessors – exploiting the profits of justice through the royal courts and via his rights over royal forests, maximizing his income from feudal payments, squeezing sheriffs for ever higher returns from their administration of the shires, and imposing one-off taxes such as scutage.

THE KING IN HIS KINGDOM

THE KING IN HIS KINGDOM

A handsome trade was done, too, in selling exemptions from royal justice or interference: the king could, and did, sell immunity from lawsuits at the shire courts, and he charged aristocratic widows vast sums for the right to remarry the man of their choice, rather than being subjected to forced marriage. Areas defined as royal forest were subjected to special royal jurisdiction, and they produced lucrative profits through fines against those who breached the forest law – this too was subjected to John's merciless attention. None of these measures were wholesale innovations: all had their roots in the earlier twelfth century, if not before. What made John's reign different was the sheer scale and relentlessness with which he bled his realm. Over the course of his reign, John's average annual income was at least £37,483 – far higher than either his father or his brother had ever achieved.[5] But his need was great.

John attempted to invade France in the early summer of 1205, and then in 1206. Neither mission was successful. In the first instance, the English barons refused to turn out in support of the king's invasion fleet, and in the second John was kept firmly at bay by the armies of Philip Augustus and had to settle for a two-year truce. Yet the Plantagenet king never gave up believing that he was obliged – perhaps even destined – to one day return to the lands he had lost and reclaim them. The consequences of this urge for revenge and restoration would be very severe, both for John and for the English kingdom in which he was now so firmly stuck.

5

INTERDICT AND INTIMIDATION

1206–1212

The ten years that followed the loss of Normandy saw John achieve a form of mastery over England and the British Isles that, although brief, was scarcely bettered by any medieval king after him. Hobbled in France as he may have been, John made it his business to stamp his authority over Wales and Scotland, to plunder and command the English Church, and to impose his will on the barons under his authority. If he did not exactly make himself popular or well-loved he nevertheless grew into his role as a fearsome lord. By the end of the first decade of the thirteenth century, the chronicler Walter of Coventry could write that 'in Ireland, Scotland and Wales there was no man who did not obey the nod of the King of England – a thing, which it is well known, had never happened to any of his forefathers'.[1] For a time, at least, John was supreme. But beneath the mastery, he was continuing to amass serious problems.

The area of policy that earned John the most infamy among the monastic chroniclers of his day was that of his relations with the pope. Across Western Christendom, kings were engaged in a grand struggle with the papacy to mark out the extent of their control over the Church – an argument that frequently focused on the issue of ecclesiastical appointments. Kings claimed the right to appoint bishops in their own kingdoms, but popes were seldom happy to allow this and reserved their right to confirm appointments – or veto those that displeased them. Just such a debate blew up in 1206 between John and the formidable, bloody-minded Pope Innocent III.

On the death of Archbishop Hubert Walter, John had instructed the monks of Canterbury to elect as his successor the king's candidate, John de Gray, Bishop of Norwich. When Innocent learned of this he decided to act; he condemned Gray's appointment and had the Canterbury monks elect instead an Englishman by the name of Stephen Langton. This slight to John's royal majesty would have been enough on its own to offend and irritate the king. It was made worse by the fact that Langton was a star theologian of the University of Paris, who therefore belonged to a distinguished intellectual circle that had included the prolific writer John of Salisbury (1120–80) and

Henry II's ill-fated archbishop, Thomas Becket. Both of these men had been, at various times, intensely critical of the Plantagenet family and their dealings with the Church, so Langton was hardly a promising candidate for a peaceful co-existence between Church and state. Nevertheless, Innocent secured his election at Canterbury and consecrated Langton personally at Viterbo, north of Rome, in 1207.

John's rage at being thwarted was always spectacular. He was not cowed by the fact that his opponent in this instance was God's anointed vicar-in-chief. In response to Langton's consecration, John seized all the lands belonging to Canterbury and threw the monks who had dared defy him out of England. Yet, he had met in Innocent a more than worthy opponent. The pope was a reformer, a crusader and a strict clerical authoritarian. He was an unbending believer in Roman supremacy, who disliked any shows of wilfulness by mere princes. So, in response to John's heavy-handed behaviour, in March 1208 Innocent laid an Interdict on England.

An Interdict was a severe sentence. It forbade all church services, effectively placing the souls of everyone affected by it into limbo. Marriages could not be consecrated, baptisms could not take place and the dead could not be buried with the usual Christian rites. The bells of England's churches fell silent. The mass went uncelebrated. This was a punishment felt far beyond the household of the king who had invited it. Indeed, if there was one man in England who was entirely unbothered by the Interdict, it was John.

John saw his falling-out with Rome in simple terms. It was an unmissable financial opportunity. As soon as the Interdict was pronounced, John began confiscating ecclesiastical wealth, lands and property. Some of it was ransomed back to its owners; the rest was simply used to provide income for the king. Churchmen's mistresses were arrested and sold back to their unhappy lovers. The ample revenues of the Church were diverted straight into the royal coffers, and John's castles and strongholds, where he stockpiled his own money, began to fill with silver at a rate of which his ancestors could have only dreamed. This was, in short, clerical extortion on a dizzying scale.

INNOCENTI
PP III
S BENEDICTUS
INNOCENTIUS EPS SERVUS SERVORU DI. DILECTIS
PRIORI ET FRIB IUXTA
SPECU BEATI BENEDICTI REGLARE VITA SERVANTIBUS
INTER HOLOCAUSTA
VIRTUTU NULLU MAGIS EST MEDULLATU QUA
OFFERTUR ALTISSIMO DE PINGUEDINE
CARITATIS. HOC IGIT ATTENDENTES. CU OLI CAUSA DEVOTIONIS ACCESSISSEM AD LOCU
INSTITUTIONE IPIUS LAUDABILITER DNO FAMULANTES. NE PRO TEPORALIS
SPIRITUALIS OBSERVANTIE DISCIPLINA TORPERET. APOSTOLICU VOBIS SUBSIDIU
IMPENDENDU. SPERANTES ID IDE BEATISSIM BENEDICT NRE DEVOTIONIS
ET PRECIB APUD PIISSIMU PATRE ET IUSTISSIMU IUDICE COMMDABIT
NECESSITATIB PUIDERE. SEX LIBRAS USUALIS MONETE VOBIS ET SUCCESSORIB
CAMERA BEATI PETRI SINGULIS ANNIS PCIPIENDAS CONCESSIM. DONEC INALIQUO CERTO LOCO
VOBIS ESSENT UTILITER ASSIGNATE. STATUENTES UT EA QUE AD SUSTENTATIONE URAM CON
SUEVISTIS PCIPERE DE MONASTERIO SUBLACEN. VOBIS ET SUCCESSORIB URIS
MINIME NEGARENTUR. POSTMODU AUTE CU REVERSI FUISSEM
URIS AD NRAM PRESENTIA DESTINASTIS HUMILITER IMPLORANTES UT
IPSA INALIQUO CERTO LOCO DIGNAREMUR PPETUO STABILIRE. DE QUO PREFATAS
SEX LIBRAS PCIPERE VALERETIS. NOS IGITUR HABITO
ASSENSU. IA DICTAS SEX LIBRAS VOBIS ET SUCCESSORIB URIS PCIPIENDAS SINGULIS
ANNIS DE ANNUO CENSU CASTRI PORTIANI CONCEDIM
PRIVILEGIO CONFIRMAM. NULLI ERGO OMNINO HOMINU LICEAT HANC PAGINA NRE
CONCESSIONIS ET CONSTITUTIONIS
IRE. SIQUIS AUTE HOC ATTEPTARE PRESUMPSERIT INDIGNATIONE OMNIPOTENTIS
ET BEATORU PETRI ET PAULI APOSTOLORU EIUS

In 1209 Innocent attempted to sharpen his threat against the English king by personally excommunicating him – at which point every bishop in England except for two of John's closest allies left the realm. John shrugged it off – and with good reason. The author of the thirteenth-century financial manual known as the 'Red Book of the Exchequer' reckoned that the Interdict enriched John by perhaps £100,000 above and beyond his normal income – all in a matter of three years. More recently it has been estimated that around half of this sum would have come in the form of ready cash, paid not into the Exchequer but directly into John's hands via the royal chamber.[2] John's coronation oath obliged him to protect and defend the interests of the English Church. He had done nothing of the sort, but for the three or four years that followed the Interdict it scarcely seemed to matter. John was, momentarily at least, the richest English king in history.

If John's plunder had been limited to the Church, then all might have still been well. But from 1207 he was increasing his extortions more generally. A tax of a thirteenth – the heaviest of his reign – brought in nearly £60,000.[*] John claimed that this tax was levied with the agreement of 'the archbishop, bishops, abbots, priors and magnates of our kingdom'; in fact, he had taken no such advice. The levy had been conceived and agreed at a meeting with a small number of his intimates and favourites.[3]

Several other very hard taxes were levied on England's Jews, including a collective imposition of 66,000 marks in 1210. The law regarded the Jews as the king's personal property, but affection towards his charges was nowhere to be seen in John: according to the chronicler Roger of Wendover, those Jews who would not, or could not, meet the king's demands were beaten until their teeth fell out.[†] Meanwhile, the standard practices of Plantagenet

---

[*]   'Thirteenth' – a thirteenth of the value of all portable property ('movables').

[†]   Wendover was writing after John's reign, and he is generally to be treated with caution when he discusses the king's excesses; all the same, his characterization of John's harshness towards England's Jews certainly reflects attitudes and memories common during the later thirteenth century.

kingship were maintained: the profits of justice kept on rising, while feudal levies and the ruthless pursuit of indebted barons also increased steeply. It was in this respect that John's cruellest and most unpleasant side was revealed.

Many of the English barons tasted the king's disfavour during the first decade of the thirteenth century. In 1207 John confiscated the lands of the Earl of Leicester, accusing him of having failed to pay his debts. The East Anglian baron Roger Bigod found himself under such tremendous financial pressure as a result of the Crown's feudal demands that he was forced to strike a deal by which, in 1211, he paid the Exchequer £1,333 (twice the fine he was charged simply to claim his inheritance) – just to have respite from the demands for payment. In early 1214 John forced another East Anglian baron, Geoffrey de Mandeville, to agree to a monstrous fine of 20,000 marks in return for marrying Isabella of Gloucester – the king's former wife, whom he had divorced in order to marry Isabella of Angoulême. Even by the standards of his family, these were savage financial impositions. John deliberately pushed numerous barons to the brink of bankruptcy, a state in which they became highly dependent on royal favour. And no one suffered so much as the de Briouze family, whom John hounded mercilessly, combining his mastery of the royal law with his appetite for extreme and unflinching personal brutality.

William de Briouze had been a close associate of both Richard I and John. He had served as a royal sheriff and as a justice of the Eyre. He had defended royal interests in Wales and had risked his life numerous times fighting against the insurgent Welsh. He had been at the siege of Châlus-Chabrol on the day that King Richard died and had helped smooth the path for John to succeed to the Plantagenet crown instead of Arthur of Brittany. He had been with John, at Rouen, on the day Arthur disappeared and almost certainly knew what had happened to the boy. He was, in short, an impeccably reliable baron, and as reward for his loyal service he had accrued many lands and titles in England, Wales and Ireland. Yet the obvious side-effect of

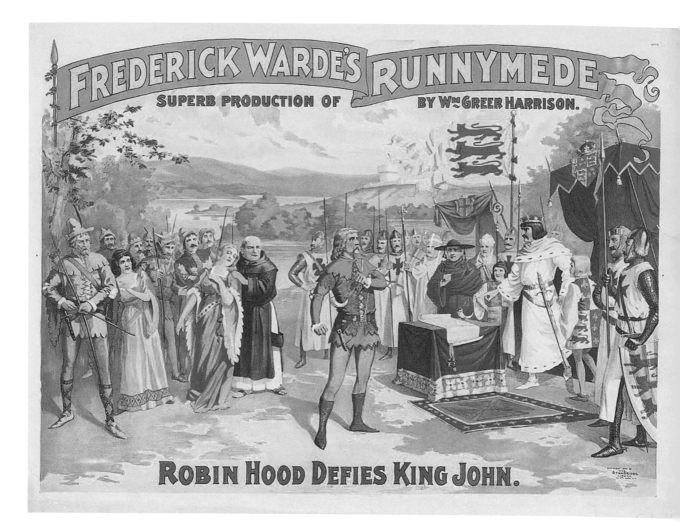

FREDERICK WARDE'S RUNNYMEDE

SUPERB PRODUCTION OF

BY Wm. GREER HARRISON.

ROBIN HOOD DEFIES KING JOHN.

INTERDICT AND INTIMIDATION

acquiring lands was the financial obligation to pay the king fees for the privilege; de Briouze was therefore entirely typical of a certain high-ranking, loyal sort of English lord, in that he had been both rewarded but also placed in enormous financial jeopardy as a result of having loyally served the Crown.

Then, in 1208, de Briouze fell out with the king. The reasons are somewhat obscure but may well have resulted from an indiscreet comment made by his wife, Matilda, concerning the suspicious circumstances of Arthur of Brittany's death. John heard – or learned of – the comments and, typically, flew into a fury. Suddenly the vast debts incurred on de Briouze's climb through Plantagenet favour became John's chief weapon with which to abuse his friend. Citing non-payment of debt, John sent his men to seize the de Briouze estates. Fearing for his life, de Briouze fled to Ireland, where he was sheltered for a time by William Marshal. John continued to pursue him, leading an army across the Irish Sea, crushing those who opposed him and seizing lands as he went. He threatened military action against those who harboured de Briouze and released an open letter in which he used tightly legalistic arguments to justify his dreadful behaviour towards a loyal man and insisting that he had acted 'according to the laws and custom of England'.[4] This may have been so, but since John's position as king allowed him to make and manipulate the law, and to enforce it prejudicially through his Exchequer, this was of little comfort to those who heard the king's claim explained. When de Briouze's wife, Matilda, approached the king to attempt to negotiate, John prevaricated, before taking Matilda and her eldest son as hostages and throwing them into one of his dungeons at Corfe Castle.

William de Briouze escaped to France, where he died an outlaw and an exile in 1211. (His funeral was attended by another exile, Archbishop Stephen Langton.) But William's fate was gentle compared to that of his family. In 1210 Matilda and her son had been starved to death on the king's orders: it was said that when the door to their cell was finally opened they were found huddled against one another in a grotesque knot of death. The mother had

died insane with hunger. Her last earthly efforts were to try and eat her child's face.

John's pursuit of the de Briouze family had taken him into Ireland and Wales, which coincided with a broader policy of muscular imposition of English royal power over the Celtic lands in Britain. From 1208 he set about attacking the native princes of North Wales, first humiliating Gwenwynwyn ap Owain, Prince of Powys, and subsequently, in 1211, launching a massive military raid into Gwynedd, smashing the power of Llywelyn ap Iorwerth (Llywelyn the Great) and commanding him to forfeit everything east of Conwy to the English Crown. This period of dominance was matched across the Irish Sea. In 1210, John's expedition in pursuit of the de Briouze family had coincided with a brutal campaign of subjection, in which Anglo-Norman and Native Irish lords alike were brought to heel, and English administrative procedures and offices were forced upon Irish territories.

In Scotland, similar ultra-aggressive methods were pursued. In 1174 Henry II had forced William I 'the Lion', King of Scots, to accept the Treaty of Falaise, under which William had explicitly recognized English overlordship of his kingdom and submitted to the English king 'as liege lord'.[5] Richard had granted independence back to the Scots in his fire-sale of rights before the Third Crusade. But in 1209 John determined to make William, aged and ill, recognize the feudal situation as it had stood thirty-five years previously. He marched an army north and forced the Lion to agree to the Treaty of Norham, under which John was paid 15,000 marks and given many Scottish hostages, including William's daughters Margaret and Isabella, whose marriages John claimed for his own sons.[6] In every corner of the British Isles, it seemed that John was supreme.

By 1212 John had done much to justify the chroniclers' opinions that he had achieved a cruel mastery over his kingdom. He was vastly, almost unimaginably, wealthy, his castles groaning with silver. He oversaw a brutally efficient legal and financial administration with which he could crush any baron who was even merely suspected of having slighted him. He had also

terrorized his neighbouring princes into submission. He appeared impervious to – even slightly amused by – the wrath of Innocent III, one of the most formidable popes ever to wear the tiara. His judicial and financial policies continued at a pace, with plans for a new Eyre to punish offences concerning the king's forest, a scheme by which debts to the Jews would be funnelled directly into the king's coffers, and an inquiry into feudal rights, which was intended to squeeze yet more value out of the king's royal prerogatives.[7] This was Plantagenet kingship at its most ruthlessly uncompromising. All that now remained for John was to return to France, try to destroy the armies and castles of King Philip Augustus and recover the lands beyond the Channel that had been lost in 1204.

It was to be his undoing.

6

CRISIS AND MACHINATIONS

1212–1214

Mighty as John must have felt in the spring of 1212, his problems with France remained firmly unresolved. The best part of a decade had passed since he had retreated to England from the shores of Normandy, yet still the duchy and the rest of his family's continental lands lay under the command of Philip Augustus. This was an intolerable situation for any Plantagenet king. To leave reconquest any longer looked like extreme idleness, not least since John had enough silver stockpiled in his English castles to invade Jerusalem if he so wished. The journey to Caen, Rouen, Le Mans and the rest was hardly prohibitively far, and the mood around the rest of Europe was right. It was time for John to make his move.

Indeed, in the spring of 1212 the potential for reconquest was growing impossible to ignore. Across Western Europe, other rulers were beginning to chafe against Philip's bullish lordship – they included the Count of Boulogne, the Duke of Brabant and others neighbouring France, including most prominently Otto of Brunswick, the son of John's sister Matilda. Otto had been raised at the court of Richard I before embarking on a spectacular political and military career in Germany and Italy, which had seen him rise to become Holy Roman Emperor (as Otto IV) in 1209. These were all serious allies, and all were interested in goading the English king into open hostility with France. Thus, in 1212 John resurrected the policy, once favoured by his brother Richard, of creating an anti-French alliance to the north and east of Philip's frontiers, all paid for handsomely with pensions and gifts to these continental friends. Then, in June, he sent out a feudal summons for an army of his own to meet at Portsmouth. Everything seemed set for an invasion. Yet it would be the moment when everything began to unravel.

John's problems began in Wales. His aggressive treatment of the native princes in 1211 returned to haunt him during the summer of 1212, in the form of a massive revolt under Llywelyn ap Iorwerth. John angrily ordered a couple of dozen Welsh hostages to be hanged, but he was still forced to divert his feudal muster from the South Coast of England to Chester, in the North-

West. Worse followed. During the summer a hermit known as Peter of Wakefield became briefly notorious for prophesying the king's death; in August the prophecy gained ominous substance, as John was told of a plot led by two of his barons – Eustace de Vesci and Robert FitzWalter – to kill him outright, or else betray him to the Welsh. John had always tended to be suspicious of his subjects, even those who considered themselves his friends. After this time, he would slip into near-constant paranoia.

Undoubtedly de Vesci and FitzWalter had their reasons for plotting against the king. Gossip of the time suggested that John had attempted to seduce both de Vesci's wife and FitzWalter's daughter. Perhaps there was some truth in this. More pertinently, though, it seems that the opposition of these two lords represented two early strains of a more general disaffection with John's reign and the whole system of Plantagenet government. De Vesci was a man of the North, a region of England that had been exposed for the first time, under John, to the full attention of a Plantagenet king, and an area that would provide many more rebel barons in the months to follow. As a group, England's Northern barons felt most aggrieved at the level of royal incursion into previously lightly governed countryside. They had the least historical interest in Normandy – which was, after all, no nearer than Norway to many of them – and most resented the provision of troops or the paying of scutage for royal expeditions across the Channel. They had the greatest sense of themselves as an independent political group whose interests over-lapped and could be threatened by outside interference.

FitzWalter was not, though, a man of the North. Rather, he was one of the wealthiest barons in East Anglia and the South-East – indeed, in the whole of England – and had been close to John for many years. He was also a quarrelsome, violent, hard-headed man. A series of relatively petty clashes with the king would appear to have pushed FitzWalter to the fore of baronial opposition, where he remained as the crisis that produced Magna Carta es-calated. He was hardly an ideologue, but he was nevertheless a product of an environment, largely of John's creation, in which the English barons had

become so disillusioned, exasperated and threatened by their king that they were prepared to countenance his murder.

De Vesci and FitzWalter both fled with their families and households, running to Scotland and France respectively, when John discovered their plot. They were outlawed in the county courts. But they were not the only plotters, and their departure neither rid the realm of trouble nor soothed the increasingly agitated mind of the king.

By 1213, then, John's position was a great deal more precarious than it had been a year previously. In aborting his invasion of France the previous summer, he had handed the military initiative to Philip Augustus, who commissioned his son and heir Louis 'the Lion' to invade England and seize the crown, and then began raising a massive fleet of his own at Damme and in the mouth of the River Zwin. The French king was emboldened by John's continued estrangement from Rome, for as an excommunicate heretic John was not protected by the pope's blessing. In fact, the situation was quite the opposite: at the beginning of 1213, Innocent III had threatened to have John deposed and sanctioned the King of France to lead a mission against him as an enemy of Christ. For all that John had been courting Philip's enemies, a counter-attack with all the righteous anger of a crusade now seemed to be imminent.

In this circumstance John showed a flash of diplomatic genius. On 13 May 1213 he met the papal legate Pandulf Verraccio, who was serving as envoy to the English court, and agreed to return to the Church, accepting Stephen Langton as Archbishop of Canterbury and – most astonishingly of all – agreeing to hand over England and Ireland as fiefs of the papacy. On 15 May he humbly submitted in public to papal overlordship, paying a mere £1,000 by way of a tribute. This was nothing to a king as flush with coin as John, and although it must have caused him some personal vexation to swallow his pride and accept an end to his extortion of the English Church, the reward was that John could now claim special protection from all of his enemies as a personal vassal of the pope.

CRISIS AND MACHINATIONS

The Battle of Bouvines on
27 July 1214, as depicted in a
detail from the fourteenth-
century manuscripts of the
Grandes Chroniques de France.
In this scene, John's ally, Count
Ferrand of Flanders, is captured.
Other allies fled the battlefield.
John effectively bet a decade's
worth of extraordinary wealth
accumulation on a campaign to
reconquer his lost French lands
in 1214. He lost.

For the English barons who opposed John, and for the French king who had been preparing to topple him from his throne, everything was now turned upside-down. The French invasion was finally seen off on 30 May when a number of English ships sneaked into the mouth of the Zwin and burned the French fleet as it bobbed at anchor there. Somehow, against all odds, John had survived a genuine crisis. But his relief would soon turn once again to despair.

For all the trouble that his plans for continental warfare had caused him, John had no intention of leaving France alone. During the rest of 1213 he continued to fund – at vast cost – a proxy war between Philip and the barons of Flanders. At the same time, he plotted his next personal invasion. Once again, however, he found that a hard core of the English barons – particularly the Northerners – were entirely unmoved by his appeals for support. Others acquiesced, sending knights and paying scutage, but they did so uneasily. On 2 November 1213, following a short military tour of the Northern counties that was designed to overawe his subjects, John held a meeting with the Northern barons at Wallingford, in Oxfordshire. There he attempted both to mollify them by promising a programme of reform, and to scare them by surrounding them with his heavily armed knights. Once this heavy-handed business was finished with, John went back to assembling a fleet and an army to take Normandy from the south. It was an awesomely grand undertaking, and John threw all he had into it. He also took more from his subjects than ever before.

In the months before his invasion of France, John extorted 10,000 marks from William FitzAlan in return for the latter's right to inherit his family's title. John de Lacy was charged 7,000 marks for a similar privilege. Widows were charged up to £1,000 to keep their dowers and to secure exemption from re-marriage. And then there was perhaps the most egregious fine of John's whole reign, in the shape of the 20,000 marks levied on Geoffrey de Mandeville for marrying John's jilted first wife. Each of these grossly inflated charges was underwritten by a promise on the payee's part

to forfeit all of his or her lands and tenements to the king if they could not keep up with payments.* Meanwhile, barons whom John suspected of disloyalty were forced to pledge lands, castles and their children as hostages as security for their good behaviour.[1] Even by John's standards this was a time of severity, mistrust, extortion and tyranny, which hardly inspired any greater love for him among his subjects. When he sailed for Poitou in February 1214, John left his castles in the North of England well garrisoned as a precaution against any immediate disquiet. He knew that his realm might spring into rebellion at any moment.

A massive campaign was planned in France, in which the English king was to march north from his base in La Rochelle, bolstered by the men of Poitou, causing sufficient distraction that Emperor Otto and John's Flemish allies could storm Paris before heading south to trap Philip Augustus's armies in a pincer movement. Yet at the crucial moment, John's Poitevin allies lost their nerve, decided against fighting the King of France, and scuttled back to their homes. John had no choice but to pitch camp and follow the news from the north.

But the news was not good. On a swelteringly hot Sunday, 27 July 1214, a coalition of John's allies – including Otto, John's illegitimate brother William Longspée (Earl of Salisbury), the counts of Boulogne and Flanders, the Duke of Brabant and assorted other expensively remunerated continental warlords – met the armies of Philip Augustus at Bouvines, a tiny village next to a bridge across the River Marcq, in what is today the Nord-Pas-de-Calais. The coalition troops rode in below a huge flag bearing Otto's emblem of a dragon and eagle. The French marched beneath their sacred banner, the *Oriflamme*. There was no question that this was a day of decisive importance. In an age of siegecraft and warfare by skirmish and attrition, full pitched battles were considered unpredictable and dangerous. They came along very infrequently indeed, and though many of the combatants would

---

*   'Tenement' – land (perhaps including property) held by the tenant of a manor.

have had experience of fighting *en masse* in the *mêlée* of the tournament field, very few would ever have taken to the battlefield for real in their whole lives. Yet all would have known that to win a battle indicated a true confirmation of God's favour.

John's allies lost at Bouvines. More than that, it was a rout. Otto and several of the other noblemen fled the field. The counts of Boulogne and Flanders and the Earl of Salisbury were captured, along with nearly thirty other high-ranking knights and noblemen and perhaps nine thousand others. For Philip Augustus, this was total vindication. 'After this, no one dared wage war against him,' wrote the chronicler known as the Anonymous of Béthune. For John, Bouvines was a catastrophe. He had gambled his reputation and most of his fortune on the outcome of a single battle in which the Almighty would speak to the rectitude of his cause. The God-given answer was that John was now a busted flush. He left French soil on 13 October and never came back.

7

A MEADOW CALLED RUNNYMEDE

1215

After the *débâcle* of Bouvines, John, his foreign-policy and military credentials now severely tarnished, returned to England to find the chorus of baronial anger at his high-handed brand of kingship louder than ever. His kingdom was teetering dangerously on the brink of civil war. It was a war he could neither avoid nor afford to pursue. John had either forsaken or exhausted his most lucrative sources of income during his preparations for the war that preceded Bouvines. Having lost that war, John had been forced – according to the chronicler Ralph of Coggeshall – to pay 60,000 marks for a five-year truce with Philip Augustus. There could not be a worse time to fund a war at home. Yet it was clear that his enemies, led by the barons of the North, expected a fight: they came armed to a conference in London in January 1215, demanding reform from the king. This worried John into taking loans from the Templars in order to raise an army of mercenaries from the continent with which he expected to have to defend his crown.[*]

Besides making desperate military preparations, John also began to seek political means by which to evade his barons' anger. His brazen actions in 1213, in raising the papal Interdict by declaring himself a liege vassal of the pope, had given him a measure of protection from Rome. On 4 March John sought to deepen his bond with Innocent III even further by taking the solemn oath of a crusader. The idea of John emulating his brother Richard and taking an army east to smash the forces of the Infidel in the Holy Land was as improbable in reality as it sounded in theory. Nevertheless, John rightly calculated that by taking crusader status he would cloak himself in yet another layer of papal favour. A man who had more or less laughed in the face of his own excommunication was now gambling that his enemies in England would not risk the same papal opprobrium by daring to attack him.

---

[*] 'Templars' – the Knights of the Temple were the earliest of Christendom's monastic military orders, their original purpose being to protect Christian pilgrims in the Holy Land. They garnered patronage and support, making them extremely wealthy.

Events, however, were moving faster even than John's devious mind. At some point between John's return from the Bouvines campaign in October 1214 and the late spring of 1215, a document known today as the 'Unknown Charter' was drawn up by those in England determined to force the king to mend his ways.[1] The Unknown Charter may reflect negotiations that were taking place between John's men and the hostile barons in early 1215. Certainly it contains the germ of much that would find its way into Magna Carta just a few months later.

The Unknown Charter begins by reciting the charter of liberties granted in 1100 by John's great-grandfather Henry I on acceding to the throne, in which Henry had promised to 'make the Holy Church of God free', to allow

his subjects to inherit on payment of a 'lawful and just' relief, to protect widows, to fix the financial penalties for crimes at some (poorly defined) ancient rate, to limit the extent of royal forests, and to keep the peace in the land in accordance with the laws of the last Saxon king, Edward the Confessor. But the Unknown Charter did not solely aim to turn back the clock 115 years. There was also a series of demands – some quite radical – which aimed to reform, or in some cases dismantle, policies that had been pillars of Plantagenet government since the beginning. These demands, written up as though the king had already assented to them, were introduced by a broad and idealistic statement, which would prove to be very close to what would become the famous clauses 39 and 40 of Magna Carta: 'King John concedes that he will arrest no man without judgment nor accept any payment for justice nor commit any unjust act.' After this, the Unknown Charter included draft commitments by the king to take only 'just reliefs' as payment for inheritance, to protect the rights of widows, to limit military service outside England to Normandy and Brittany 'and this properly', to limit scutage to one mark per knight's fee, and to return all lands that had been 'afforested' (i.e. newly declared to be royal forest) under Henry II, Richard and John.[*]

The Unknown Charter, although its date is (as its name implies) uncertain, tells us much about the thinking of John's disgruntled subjects in the months immediately prior to Magna Carta. They were not only angling to rebel against a king who had treated them roughly and who had failed in war; they were also preparing to challenge a raft of political issues that reached to the very core of the Plantagenet system of government. Whoever drew up the Unknown Charter was reading English history as a succession of perversions and betrayals committed since Henry II's accession in 1154, in which the spirit of the 'good old days' – specifically the reigns of Henry I and Edward the Confessor – had been lost. They wished to make a number of

OPPOSITE
… in prato quod vocatur Ronimed inter Windlesoram et Stanes – 'in the meadow which is called Runnymede, between Windsor and Staines'. It was here in June 1215, beside the Thames, that Magna Carta was negotiated and subsequently granted by King John. This modern memorial to that event was commissioned by the American Bar Association, a testament to the profound and widespread impact of Magna Carta in the 800 years that followed.

---

[*] 'Knights fee' – a unit of land considered sufficient to support the livelihood of a single knight for a year. Its size depended on the location and value of the land.

specific amendments to policy, setting limits to the king's ability to tax and fine his subjects. But they also sought to set out grand and sweeping philosophical statements concerning the king's basic duties towards Church and people. It is unlikely that all of the aims were shared by all of John's opponents. Some, no doubt, simply wished to be revenged on a man who had extorted, bullied, blasphemed and murdered his way through life and kingship for far too long. But others – and there were without doubt many – saw in the immediate crisis of 1215 a chance to change their world in a more fundamental way. It was the alliance of these interests that would make the baronial reform movement of 1215 irresistible.

*

On the great tournament field in Brackley, Northamptonshire, on 5 May 1215 a group of barons formally renounced their fealty – their feudal loyalty – to King John. It was ten days since John had failed to appear at a scheduled conference at Northampton, where he had been due to reply to a set of demands that were probably very like those laid out in the Unknown Charter. By abandoning their oath of duty to the king, the barons were effectively declaring themselves free to make war upon him. It was a position from which they would find it hard to retreat.

On 9 and 10 May John offered to submit to various forms of arbitration – either by the advice of men he considered faithful, or by his own courts, or else by a panel of eight barons convened under the ultimate authority of the pope. None of these was deemed acceptable by the rebellious barons, so on 12 May John ordered his men to lay siege to rebel castles. This was war. And England's great men were now forced to choose sides. Did they stand behind a crusader king with the backing of the pope, who had offered peace, albeit on terms weighted heavily in his favour? Or did they take up arms against a tyrant who had oppressed them, and would no doubt continue to do so if left unchecked?

A good number chose the path of loyalty, seeing that to oppose a king with the backing of Rome was a risky business, and that the alternative to obedience was anarchy. William Marshal, Earl of Pembroke, had been a servant of the Plantagenets since John was born and, despite having fallen out with the king over the de Briouze affair, was not prepared to turn against him. Nor were other great men such as William, Earl Warenne. John also had by his side a man who spoke with the pope's authority: Pandulf Verraccio. Nevertheless, ranged against the king and his supporters was a very formidable coalition of the disaffected. It included the plotters of 1212, Eustace de Vesci and Robert FitzWalter; the latter had decided to adopt the pompous title of Marshal of the Army of God. Alongside them were more recognized 'Northerners' – men like William de Mowbray, Richard de Percy and Roger de Montbegon – and other major landowners based elsewhere in the country, such as Roger Bigod, Earl of Norfolk; Robert de Vere, Earl of Oxford; and Saer de Quincy, Earl of Winchester (who had, until January 1215, been one of John's closest advisers). Crucially, the rebels also included the men of London. The City gates were opened to rebels under FitzWalter on Sunday 17 May – a deed apparently done by trickery while many of the citizens were occupied at mass.

Between the king and the rebels – although clearly leaning towards the latter – sat Stephen Langton, the archbishop who had been at the root of so many of John's earlier problems. Langton would be an important mediator, and would subsequently make a profound intellectual contribution to the final charter that appeared in June 1215.[2]

With London under rebel command, John was forced to turn to negotiation, for he could not very well take England's capital, stoutly defended and packed with his enemies, by siege. Therefore, shortly after London fell to rebel control, John issued warrants of safe conduct for Saer de Quincy and Archbishop Langton, allowing them to approach him as baronial diplomats. On 29 May he again offered unsuccessfully to submit to papal arbitration. By now the king was staying in the area around Windsor, half a day's ride

upriver from London. And by the first week of June a regular meeting place for the king's party and the barons had been established. A few miles south-east of Windsor was a large meadow, which today stands green and lush, shaded by tall leafy oak trees, flanked by the slow-moving Thames on one side and low, gently sloping hills on the other. This is the place that Magna Carta refers to as *in prato quod vocatur Ronimed, inter Windlesoram et Stanes* – 'the meadow called Runnymede between Windsor and Staines'. For the first week and a half of June, messengers rode back and forth to, and through, this meadow, travelling between the king's party and the barons in London. They were toiling their way towards a solution to the stand-off – a means by which the full horror of civil war could be avoided. And slowly but surely the skeleton of a peace treaty began to form.

The exact sequence of events during the days that led up to the agreement and production of Magna Carta, and to the proclamation of peace between king and barons that it allowed, remains muddied by the uncertainty of 800 years' distance.[3] But a sensible reconstruction of events would seem to be as follows.

From the end of May 1215 both John and his barons accepted that peace had to be made, on something loosely similar to the terms of the Unknown Charter. For the next ten days the deal between the sides was drafted and redrafted by royal clerks. One such draft – clearly very close to a final version of Magna Carta – survives in the form of a document that was authenticated with the king's Great Seal and which Langton subsequently seems to have kept safe for posterity: this document is known as 'The Articles of the Barons'.[4] Unlike the Unknown Charter, it no longer included a copy of Henry I's concessions. But on matters of immediate dispute between king and barons it was much more sophisticated and detailed. It ran to forty-nine clauses, each of which went into considerable technical detail about the rates of reliefs for inheritance, widows' rights, the treatment of debtors to the Crown, levels for scutage, feudal aids and rents, the extent to which certain writs could be used by the Crown, procedures for dealing with debts to

Jewish lenders – and more, down to apparently trivial matters of reform such as weights and measures, the protocol for funding the rebuilding of bridges, and the placement of fish-weirs along the rivers Thames and Medway.

The Articles of the Barons also included the statement that 'the body of a free man be not arrested or disseized or outlawed or exiled or in any way victimized, nor shall the king attack or send anyone to attack him by force, except by the judgment of his peers or by the law of the land'.* Just as with the Unknown Charter, it is clear that the king's enemies were feeling their way now very closely towards a generalized statement that would commit the king to refraining from tyranny. Equally importantly, the Articles included the draft of what would become Magna Carta's most ambitious clause of all: a security clause (61). This proposed to set up a council of twenty-five barons who would effectively become the trustees of the peace, empowered by law to respond to royal breaches of the law by 'distrain[ing] and distress[ing] the king in all ways possible'.

The negotiations at Runnymede were not easy, and the whole process was almost certainly extremely irksome to John, whose mood is captured – perhaps fancifully, but quite believably all the same – by the Benedictine chronicler Matthew Paris, who wrote that when the king was entreating with his opponents he behaved calmly, but behind the scenes 'he gnashed his teeth, rolled his eyes, grabbed sticks and straws and gnawed them like a madman'. However, if John did rage privately in this way it was pointless. By Wednesday 10 June, the broad terms of the Articles of the Barons had been accepted by both sides, and John had extended his peace to the barons until the following Monday morning, 15 June. This delay probably served two purposes. In the first place it gave time for the interested parties – the king, the various voices within the rebel faction, and the representatives of the Church, led by Stephen Langton – to iron out remaining wrinkles within the

---

* 'Disseize' – to strip someone of their land or property holdings .

Post decessum antecessorum heredes plene etatis habebunt hereditatem suam per antiquum relevium exprimend' in carta.

Heredes infra etatem sunt et fuerunt in custodia cum ad etatem pervenerint: habeant hereditatem suam sine relevio et sine fine.

Custos terre heredis capiat rationabiles exitus consuetudines et servicia sine destructione et vasto hominum et rerum suarum et si custos ille fecerit destructionem et vastum inde amittat custodiam et custos sustentabit domos parcos vivaria stagna molendina et cetera ad eandem terram pertinentia de exitibus terre eiusdem et ut heredes ita maritentur ne disparagentur et per consilium propinquorum de consanguinitate sua.

Ne vidua det aliquid pro dote sua vel pro maritagio post decessum mariti sui si vivere velit in domo sua per quadraginta dies post mortem ipsius et infra eundem terminum illam assignetur ei dos sua et rationabilem estoverium habeat et hereditatem suam.

Nec vel Balli' non saisiet terram aliquam pro debito dum catalla debitoris sufficiant nec plegii debitoris distringantur dum capitalis debitor sit suf' ad solvend' et si vero capitalis debitor defecerit in solutione si plegii voluerint habeant terras et debitorem donec debitum illud persolvatur plene nisi capitalis debitor monstrare poterit se de eo quietum erga plegios.

Non concedet alii Baroni ut capiat auxilium de liberis hominibus suis nisi ad corpus suum redimendum et ad faciend' primogenitum filium suum militem et ad primogenitam filiam suam semel maritandam et hoc faciet per rationabile auxilium.

Ne aliquis maiorem districtionem faciat de feodo militis quam inde debetur.

Ne communia placita sequantur curiam domini Regis set assignentur in aliquo certo loco et ut recognitiones capiantur in eadem Comitatibus hoc medio ut Rex mittet duos iusticiarios per quatuor vices in anno qui cum quatuor militibus eiusdem Comitatus electis per Comitatum capiant assisas de nova disseisina morte antecessoris et ultima presentatione nec aliquis ob hoc ire cogatur.

Ne liber homo amercietur pro parvo delicto nisi secundum modum delicti et pro magno delicto secundum magnitudinem delicti salvo contenemento suo et villanus alterius quam noster eodem modo salva merchandisa sua et pertinentum per sacramentum proborum hominum de visneto.

Ne etiam amercietur de cetero ferdas suas secundum modum alterius forisfacti et non secundum voluntatem curie.

Ne aliqua villa amercietur pro pontibus faciendis ad riparias nisi ubi de iure antiquitus esse solebant.

De mensuris vini et bladi et latitudine pannorum et rebus aliis emendetur et idem de ponderibus.

Ne assisa de Nova disseisina et de morte antecessoris abbrevietur sed amplietur de aliis assisis.

De nullo brevi intromittat se de placito ad coronam pertinente sive curia cum Comitatus et hundredi sint ad annis firma absque nullis incrementis exceptis antiquis incrementis.

Si quis tenens de Rege moriatur licebit vicecomiti vel alii Ballivo Regis saisire et imbreviare catalla ipsius per visum legalium hominum ita tamen quod nichil inde amoveatur donec persolvatur debitum Regis et tunc debitum Regi persolvatur residuum vero relinquatur executoribus ad faciend' testamentum defuncti et si nichil Regi debeatur catalla cedant defuncto.

Si aliquis liber homo intestatus decesserit bona sua per manus parentum propinquorum suorum et amicorum per visum ecclesie distribuantur.

Ne vidua distringatur ad se maritand' dum voluerit sine marito vivere ita quod securitatem faciet quod non maritabitur sine assensu Regis si de Rege tenuerit vel sine dominorum suorum de quibus tenuerit.

Ne Constabularius vel alius Ballivus capiat blada vel alia catalla nisi statim denarios reddat nisi respectum inde habere possit de voluntate venditoris.

Ne Constabularius possit distringere aliquem militem ad dandum denarios pro custodia castri si ipse velit facere custodiam illam per se vel per alium probum hominem si ipse eam facere non possit pro rationabili causa et si Rex eum duxerit in exercitu proficiscens de custodia sit quietus secundum quantitatem temporis.

Ne vel Ballivus Regis vel aliquis alius capiat equos vel carettas alicuius liberi hominis pro cariagio faciendo nisi ex voluntate ipsius.

Ne Rex vel Ballivus suus capiat alienum boscum ad castra vel ad alia agenda sua nisi per voluntatem ipsius cuius boscus ille fuerit.

Ne Rex teneat terram eorum qui fuerint convicti de felonia nisi per annum et unum diem et tunc reddatur terra dominis feodorum.

De omnibus kidellis de cetero penitus deponendis de Tamisia et Medeweya et per totam Angliam.

Ne breve quod vocatur precipe de cetero fiat alicui de aliquo tenemento unde liber homo amittere possit curiam suam.

Si quis fuerit disseisitus vel elongatus per Regem sine iudicio de terris libertatibus sive iure suo statim ei restituatur et si contentio super hoc orta fuerit tunc per iudicium viginti quinque Baronum de quibus fit mentio inferius in securitate pacis et si aliquis fuerit disseisitus per patrem vel fratrem suum rectum habeat sine dilatione per iudicium parium suorum in Curia Regis et si Rex debeat habere terminum aliorum crucesignatorum tunc Archiepiscopus Cantuariensis inde iudicium et cetera eorum decem adiutorem removeat.

Si aliquis tenuerit per feodum firmam per socagium vel per burgagium et de alio per servicium militis non habeat Rex custodiam heredis nec terre sue que est de feodo alterius occasione illius burgagii vel socagii sed nec habeat custodiam illius burgagii vel socagii vel feodi firme et non amittat ille custodiam militie occasione alicuius parve servicii per manualium hominum de eo qui tenet aliquid tenementum reddendo inde cultellos vel sagittas vel huiusmodi.

Ne aliquis Ballivus ponat aliquem ad legem simplici loquela sua sine testibus fidelibus.

Ne corpus liberi hominis capiatur nec imprisonetur nec disseisietur nec utlagetur nec exuletur nec aliquo modo destruatur nec Rex eat vel mittet super eum vi nisi per iudicium parium suorum vel per legem terre.

Ne vendat vel differat aut vetet aliquid rectum vel iusticiam.

Ut mercatores habeant salvum ire et venire ad emendum vel vendendum sine omnibus malis toltis per antiquas et rectas consuetudines.

Si quisquam vel aliquid tenuerit per feod' firmam per socagium vel per burgagium et de alio per socagium vel per burgagium et de alio per servicium militis habeat custodiam heredis feodi.

terms of the proposed peace. In the second place it allowed time for all to prepare for a gathering that was larger and nobler than the meetings between envoys that had been taking place until that point. This was to be the formal and final creation of the treaty – the agreement that we now call Magna Carta.

If we believe what is stated in King John's voice at the end of each of the four surviving copies of the 1215 Magna Carta, then Monday 15 June was the day on which the great charter was 'given by our hand'. In other words, this is the day upon which Magna Carta came into being, and on which the first copies of the document were produced. Despite what is often supposed, Magna Carta was never 'signed', in the manner of the great peace treaties of the twentieth century. It was 'given' (i.e. formally assented to by the king), 'engrossed' (i.e. written up on a large piece of parchment in a fair hand, so that it might easily be read by others and reproduced by chancery clerks) and certified by the attachment of the royal seal. These three stages were part of a single process, and they probably happened on 15 June.

Yet this was not the end to the peace-making. It was only on the Friday of the same week, 19 June, that the rebellious barons assembled before the king and renewed the homage that they had abandoned at Brackley, thereby signalling their acceptance of the terms in the charter that the king had given. We may assume that the four days that elapsed between 15 and 19 June were taken up on the rebel side by arguments over whether to accept the deal that had been put in front of them or not. Clearly, a large number of the barons did so. But some did not. For certain men, particularly hardline Northerners, the king remained a tyrant and an enemy, and his charter was not worth the parchment it was written on. These hardliners returned to the North in disgust and prepared to fight on against a king they would never learn to trust. In a sense, they were right. Within six weeks John had overturned the deal that was made at Runnymede and the war that everyone had tried to avoid was sweeping through England.

8

A CHARTER OF LIBERTIES

MAGNA CARTA
1215

Four parchment versions, 'engrossments', of the Magna Carta as assented to by John on 15 June 1215 at Runnymede survive today. Two are held in the British Library (one of them badly damaged by a fire in 1731, although it still has its seal attached); a third is held in Salisbury Cathedral, and a fourth belongs to Lincoln Cathedral and is kept nearby in the secure environment of Lincoln Castle. There are small variations between the four documents – including an unusual handwriting style used in the Salisbury copy – but essentially all are replica agreements, and all would once have carried the solemn royal stamp of authenticity in the form of a large, double-sided waxen seal attached to the bottom of the document with a short length of silk cord.

There would once have been many more copies of the 1215 Magna Carta – and indeed, many copies and later reissues of the charter survive in archives across the world. But precisely how many more of the 'original' charters once existed is unknown. It is also hard to say if there was ever one original 'master' document sealed in the sort of ceremony which is often romantically imagined, painted or re-enacted. In fact, we must probably abandon altogether the image of King John seated before his great document, a medieval version of a modern footballer about to sign a lucrative playing contract. No king of John's era would have stooped to such a lowly task as sealing his own documents. This was a specialized task carried out by a member of the Chancery called a spigurnel.[1] Magna Carta was most likely agreed in its terms, symbolically put into action with the renewal of the barons' homage to John on 19 June and then distributed to the counties and towns of England during the last days of the month. The process of making peace and agreeing constitutional principles was messy, and it took time.

Ragged as this aspect of Magna Carta's history and mythology may be, the contents of the charter were still extremely significant, as would have been very obvious to all who read the charter – or more commonly, heard it read aloud to them. Its words – more than 4,000 of them, in Latin – dealt with a vast wealth of political, legal, judicial, ecclesiastical, economic and

feudal matters, often in great detail. Although the original charter was in continuous prose, it is now customary to subdivide it into clauses (or chapters), of which there are sixty-three (*see* Appendix I). Read in sequence, they feel like a great jumble of issues and statements that barely follow one from the other. Read together, however, they form a critique of almost every aspect of Plantagenet kingship in general and the rule of John in particular.

Magna Carta begins with a preamble, in which John, still claiming his titles of Duke of Normandy and Aquitaine and Count of Anjou, addresses all the great men of his kingdom – 'archbishops, bishops, abbots, earls, barons' – as well as his own servants – 'justices, foresters, sheriffs, reeves ... [and] bailiffs.'[2] Innocuously, but very importantly, the charter is also addressed to *omnibus ... fidelibus suis* – to all John's 'faithful subjects'. This faithfulness is crucial. The charter that follows this introduction is about granting the king's peace and the confirmation of many long-desired liberties. But these two privileges, it is made plain, are only to be enjoyed by those who submit to John's rule, accepting his lordship and – where necessary – seeking reconciliation. No one could have fooled themselves that John was granting Magna Carta to his people with an entirely glad and open heart. All the same, by drawing on the term *fidelus* John was ensuring that this was an agreement that traded some quite serious dents to his royal prerogative for unequivocal submission on the part of his enemies.

Next comes a list of those men whom John says have advised him on the document. There are twenty-seven names in total (*see* Appendix II), most of whom were bishops and barons who had remained loyal during the stand-off of the preceding weeks. These men are also named in Clause 62 as the witnesses to the charter. At the top of the list was Archbishop Stephen Langton, 'Primate of all England and Cardinal of the Holy Roman church'. Langton had, of course, been the prime mediator at Runnymede. It is therefore appropriate that the opening clause of Magna Carta is the one that most obviously bore his stamp:[3]

Firstly, we have granted to God and confirmed by this, our present charter, for us and our heirs in perpetuity, that the English Church shall be free.

These first words, of the first clause, are of immense importance, for here was an attempt by Langton to settle for good the argument that had raged between Plantagenet kings and their archbishops ever since Henry II and Thomas Becket first clashed in the 1160s. Generally speaking, the reference to the Church and its liberties echoed the opening remarks of Henry I's coronation charter, which had been a formative influence on Magna Carta.[4] More specifically, Langton was securing from the king a promise to avoid interfering in Church elections – and clearly Langton's personal experience gave him ample cause for this. Yet just as important is the fact that at the end of this clause, once his vows to refrain from meddling with the Church have been made, John effectively re-introduces the charter, stating that 'we have also granted to all the free men of our realm … all the liberties written below'. John's contract with the Church and with his lay subjects was therefore separated. His promises to the Church were placed above all others – awarded pre-eminence and perhaps even special protection.

In the earlier Articles of the Barons there was no mention anywhere of Church freedom. In Magna Carta, by contrast, the issue is elevated above all others. Langton's hand, late in the negotiations, had lifted his own political concerns directly to the top of the list. And for the avoidance of doubt of the special place in which John's promises to the Church were to be regarded, the sixty-third and final clause restates the fact: 'we wish and firmly command that the English Church shall be free and that men in our kingdom have and hold all the aforesaid liberties'. Magna Carta is often thought to be a document concerned with the secular rights of subjects or citizens – yet in 1215 its religious considerations were given pride of place.

Next, Magna Carta deals with one of the biggest issues of dispute between John and his barons: that of reliefs for inheritance. Here, John agrees to limit his demands for allowing earls, barons and the kingdom's other great

men to inherit to '£100 for the whole barony' or 100 marks in the case of a knight. No longer would men like William FitzAlan be charged outlandish sums like 10,000 marks to have their inheritance. No longer, equally, was John to be allowed to force his great men into effective bankruptcy as a means of political control. No more were John's bailiffs to 'seize any land … for any debt, so long as the debtor's chattels are sufficient to pay the debt' (Clause 9). The process for assessing the wealth of the freshly dead – and therefore the inheritance tax due to the king – was spelled out, in an attempt to blunt the teeth of aggressive royal officials (clauses 26 and 27). In other words, the power of the Exchequer – which had grown markedly under John – to extort, bully, and ruin anyone whom the king happened merely to dislike, was now placed under strict supervision.

Other major political issues can be traced throughout Magna Carta. The county 'farm' – the fixed tax taken by royal sheriffs – was to be fixed at its 'ancient' (*antiquas*) rates, although what these rates would be is not defined (Clause 25). The occasions on which the king could take scutage – the military tax John had levied eleven times during his relatively short reign – were limited to paying a ransom for his person, 'the knighting of our first-born son or the first marriage of our first-born daughter' (Clause 12). Much more importantly, in terms of England's later constitutional development at least, was the promise that the king would only take scutage at a 'reasonable' rate and after taking 'the common counsel of our realm' (*per commune consilium regni nostri*) – counsel which was to be summoned according to a newly defined protocol in Clause 14. During the later thirteenth and fourteenth centuries, the notion that tax was only to be taken when the kingdom had agreed on it – in Parliament, as the formal meetings between king and subjects later became known – would emerge as one of the most sacred ideas in English political thought and practice.

Other clauses in the charter dealt with different aspects of the law and custom of inheritance. Widows (in clauses 7 and 8) were to have their 'marriage portion and inheritance straight away and without difficulty' and

A CHARTER OF LIBERTIES

without being forced to pay the king a fine for the privilege, and they would not be forced to marry against their will. (Magna Carta was not entirely liberal-minded with regard to women, however – Clause 54 stated that 'no man shall be arrested or imprisoned because of the appeal of a woman for the death of anyone but her husband.') Young men (Clause 3) who were under the legal age of majority at the time that they inherited their lands were not to be charged fees to come into their inheritance when they grew up, and the king agreed not to seize young men and claim them as his wards without good feudal reason (Clause 37). Men who were granted the wardship of such young heirs were to treat their parks, woods and farmland with respect and diligence, preserving the inheritance rather than simply milking the land for quick profit (clauses 4 and 5).

Other issues touched upon in Magna Carta included debt to Jewish moneylenders, and the king was forbidden from taking over high-interest loans and pursuing the interest on them with his own officials (clauses 10 and 11). London – whose citizens had played such an important role in bringing John to the point of negotiation with his enemies – had its ancient liberties confirmed 'both on land and on water' (Clause 13) and the City's merchants were granted freedom of movement and an exemption from 'evil tolls' (*malis toltis*) in clauses 41 and 42. The Court of Common Pleas – the highest court in the land – was to have a fixed home, rather than requiring people seeking justice to find John wherever his caravan court might then be resting. County courts were also to be held at fixed times and in fixed places throughout the year (clauses 17–19) and the fines (known as 'amercements') that they imposed for offences were to be reasonable (clauses 20–22). Clause 23 regulated bridge-building, while Clause 33 banned fish weirs – the wooden traps that blighted river transport – from the Thames and Medway. In Clause 35 weights and measures were regulated for the most important things in life: corn, cloth and ale. Magna Carta forbade the hated practice of purveyance – by which royal officials, and particularly the garrisons of the king's many castles up and down the land, took goods,

crops, horses and carts for the king's use without paying (or intending to pay) for them (clauses 28, 30 and 31.) And it touched briefly upon the contentious laws of the English forest, pledging not to use forest judges to try men who lived outside forest land (Clause 44), to investigate corruption among forest officials (Clause 48), and to reverse the creep of forest boundaries that had taken place in John's reign (Clause 47) – although, crucially, not that which had taken place under Henry II and Richard I.

As well as these specific reforms, Magna Carta dealt, of course, in grand ideas. Indeed, it is thanks to its broadest – and in some ways least politically successful – clauses that Magna Carta has remained famous for eight centuries. Earls and barons were only to be 'amerced' (fined) 'by their peers' and 'in accordance with the nature of the offence' (Clause 21). Judges, sheriffs and other royal officials were to be competent (Clause 45). Later, the charter expands the principle further, in what is perhaps one of most enduring clauses of any major constitutional document in the last thousand years:

No free man is to be arrested, or imprisoned, or disseized, or outlawed, or exiled, or in any other way ruined, nor will we go or send against him, except by the legal judgment of his peers or by the law of the land [nisi per legale judicium parium suorum]

In 1215 this statement, from Clause 39, was designed (albeit rather impractically) to stop John's highly personal and arbitrary pursuit of his greatest men. Over the years, however, Clause 39 – in tandem with the next clause, which simply states of the king that 'to no one will we sell, to no one will we deny or delay, right or justice' – has been taken to enshrine the principles of trial by jury, Habeas Corpus and the basic idea that justice should always restrain the power of government.

Yet for everything that was grand and far-reaching in Magna Carta, there was much that remained vague, woolly or fudged. In places, Magna Carta feels like frustratingly unfinished business. Clauses such as 'no one is

One of the four surviving copies of Magna Carta as granted in 1215. This is one of the two held at the British Library; the others are owned by Salisbury and Lincoln cathedrals respectively. Written on parchment, which is derived from sheepskin, its closely written Latin has many of its words abbreviated. There would have originally been many more copies in 1215, since once granted and 'engrossed', Magna Carta was replicated and distributed across England.

to be distrained to do more service for a knight's fee . . . than is owed for it' (Clause 16) were clearly pushing towards much more complex political issues: in this case, the issue at stake was John's practice of insisting on military service or payment from those whose feudal tenure did not, in fact, require them to give it. But – perhaps due to the pressures of time or the intractability of negotiators – such issues were diplomatically abandoned, the bones of an idea left unfleshed. The king promised to 'immediately restore all hostages and charters that have been given to us by Englishmen as security for peace and faithful service' (Clause 49) and to expel both named individuals and 'all foreign knights, crossbowmen, serjeants and mercenaries' (clauses 50 and 51) – although how or where this decommissioning process was to take place was left unspoken.

In other places, King John's manifest duplicity fairly leaps from the ancient parchment: the king promised to restore 'lands, castles, liberties [and] rights' to those whom he had maltreated (Clause 52), whether in England or Wales (Clause 56), yet in the case of dispute, or of complaints from his subjects that dated back to the reigns of Henry II and Richard I (clauses 53 and 57), the cases were to be adjourned for the duration of John's crusade. Whether or not John really intended to leave England to torment the Infidel instead of his own subjects we may doubt. Surely many at the time did. Nevertheless, the king was protected as much as he was obligated by the crusader's cross he had taken up in March 1215. He used the fact to wriggle as much as he possibly could.

John's capacity for wriggling had obviously escaped no one involved in the making of Magna Carta, and it was for this reason that the most important clause of all was added to the agreement. Attention is often lavished on clauses 39 and 40 by those seeking in Magna Carta the foundation stones of Western democracy. But equally significant is Clause 61, for it is this, known as the 'security' [*securitatem*] clause, by which the men of 1215 sought to find some way to hold the king to his own word, as given in the charter. For, quite clearly, all the fine efforts in bringing the king to Runnymede, persuading

him to grant the charter and having it sent far and wide across the country would come to nothing if John decided simply to break his promises and return to the mode of kingship he preferred: overbearing, extortionate and cruel.

The security clause sets up what must have seemed like a sensible enough scheme to tie the king to his word. If the king were to 'transgress against any of the articles of peace', a panel of twenty-five specially elected barons (*see* Appendix III) was entitled, under the terms of the charter, to 'distrain and distress us in all ways possible, by taking castles, lands and possessions and in any other ways they can … saving our person and the persons of our queen and children'. If the king backslid, he would find himself under attack by his own subjects. Or to put it more simply, Magna Carta allowed for licensed civil war.

And yet here lay the great contradiction at the heart of Magna Carta. The barons had attempted for the first time in English history to create a mechanism that allowed the community of the realm to override the king's universal authority when that same authority was abused. This would be the aim of many generations of rebels after them. But as they found, this was no easy task. In 1215 a document that was intended as a peace treaty ended up sanctioning a return to war. Indeed, it may be said that Magna Carta made war *more* and not less likely, for its explicit mechanism of enforcement was to invoke a large-scale baronial revolt of the sort that the charter was designed to halt! How could this possibly be a recipe for peace? Even as the barons renewed their homage on 19 June it was probably not obvious in their minds whether, or how, the agreement was really going to work.

All this notwithstanding, it remains true that John had been forced at Runnymede to issue a longer and more comprehensive statement of what purported to be English law and custom than had been demanded or received from any of his predecessors. It combined detailed legal process with grand pronouncements about relations between Church and Crown and king and subjects. If any one idea could be said to run beneath or through

The Great Seal of King John. Once Magna Carta was granted, the royal seal would have been applied to the various copies then produced by industrious scribes. Only one of the four surviving 1215 copies, at the British Library, still has remnants of its seal. Unfortunately, that copy is also partially burnt, the result of a fire at the Westminster home of Sir Robert Cotton in 1731, when it was still part of the collection that he later bequeathed to the nation.

all the clauses of Magna Carta, it is that which had been expressed by the theologian John of Salisbury in his *Policraticus*, composed almost six decades previously, in 1159. Salisbury compared a prince with a tyrant and concluded that the essential difference between the two was that while both *made* and *enforced* laws, the prince also *subjected* himself to the law.[5] This was a law that the king granted but that the free people of England (rich men, mostly) owned jointly as the community of the realm. Magna Carta was simultaneously an attempt to reach agreement between king and barons about what the existing laws of the land were (as defined by 'custom'), to spell out some more general spirit in which new laws should be made, and – perhaps most importantly of all – to find some formula by which the king could be forced to stick to what he had agreed.

Unfortunately, it was this third element of enforcing Magna Carta that caused it to fail almost immediately. Yet, in searching for a way to restrain a powerful monarch, King John's enemies had begun to seek an answer to the basic constitutional question that would return to preoccupy England repeatedly during the Middle Ages.

9

WAR AND INVASION
1215–1216

For all its ambitions and fine words, in 1215 Magna Carta was a failure. It failed to keep the peace. It failed to bind the king to the letter of the law or to any more elevated principles of government. It failed to reconcile John with the Northerners. It was annulled by the pope within weeks of its promulgation, and England was soon to be swallowed up by a civil war that brought back memories of the darkest days of the Anarchy. In immediate political terms, therefore, the charter was a disaster. Eventually, Magna Carta would rise to become one of the most revered documents, both of the Middle Ages and of eight centuries of English history. But there would have been few people willing to bet on that that during the autumn of 1215.

If John had ever entertained the slightest intention of sticking to the terms of Magna Carta – and this is far from certain – he had abandoned it by July, when he wrote to Pope Innocent III requesting that the charter be annulled. He claimed that its terms had been extracted from him under duress and were, as a result, not binding. The pope, as John's overlord and crusading sponsor, was only too happy to agree. By September 1215, papal letters had been delivered to England, expressing Innocent's strong indignation that a vassal of his should be treated so by mere subjects, and releasing John from his obligation to obey the terms of the charter. Pope Innocent took a bombastic tone from the start:

Although our well-beloved son in Christ, John illustrious King of the English, grievously offended God and the Church ... the king at length returned to his senses ... But the enemy of the human race [i.e. Satan] *who always hates good impulses, by his cunning wiles stirred up against him the barons of England so that, with a wicked inconstancy, the men who supported him when injuring the Church rebelled against him when he turned from his sin ...* [1]

...uim anni machinamur uoi uentete dignouui. apud landsui
cum de nauibz exiens. puinciam totam prer douense ca
strum sibi continuo subiugauit. Dein londonias ueniens.
cum ingenti omnium baronum leticia suscepr̄ ē. Cepit itz
homagia ⁊ fidelitatem ab omnibz baronibz ac ciuibz qui
ibidem expectauerant ipsius aduentum. Ille uero tactis
sacrosctīs euūgelus iurauit qz singulis eorum bonas legē
redderent. simul ⁊ amissas hereditates. Scripsit etiam rogī

⁊ it͟ iii londoñ
dirigens castrū
Rofense ⁊ sūa re
cepit potestatē

...ca ⁊ bm. s.
vbiii kl' se
ad ulciora dire
cta etiā cōten
puicīa sine dif
ficultate sibi
oīnus subiugau͟

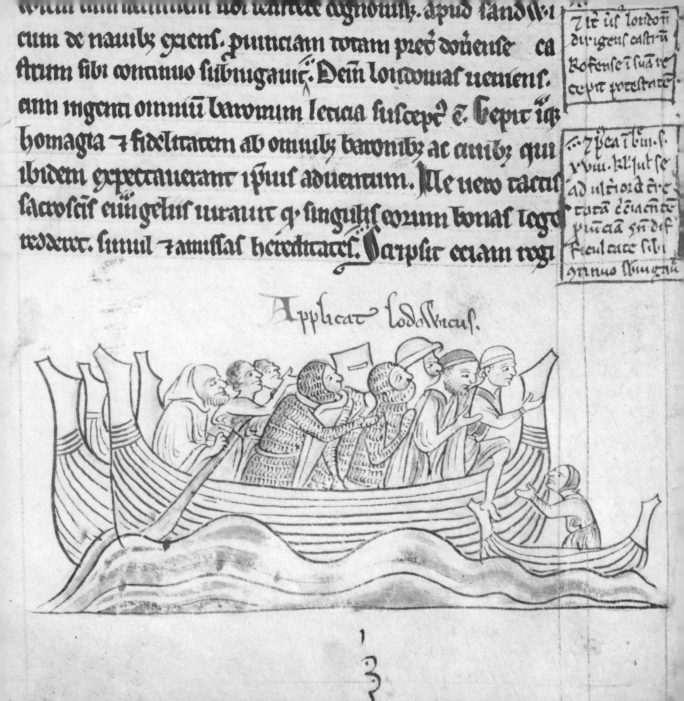

Applicat Lodowicus.

Innocent accused the barons of having thrown over their oaths of fealty, 'conspiring as vassals against their lord and as knights against their king … and dared to make war on him, occupying and devastating his territory and even seizing the City of London, which had been treacherously surrendered to them'. The barons were accused of being unreasonable, treacherous and truculent, of exhibiting such 'shameless presumption' that 'the king's rights [were] injured, the English nation shamed and the whole plan for a crusade seriously endangered'. The pope concluded by saying that 'we utterly reject and condemn this settlement [Magna Carta] and under threat of excommunication we order that the king should not dare to observe it and that the barons and their associates should not require it to be observed'. Magna Carta was 'null, and void of all validity forever'. Nine barons and all the citizens of London were excommunicated, for good measure.

This was hardly a gesture of goodwill. As a result, civil war resumed. By now, many of the English barons had given up believing that John might be reformed, tamed or otherwise controlled. Certainly, John's own behaviour did not suggest a penitent soul: he had taken to threatening Archbishop Langton (who held Rochester Castle and refused to give it up, resulting in its siege), and from 17 September he was seizing baronial property by force. John's opponents therefore began once again to resist his rule. Royal officials were ignored or replaced with the barons' own men. All money owed to the Crown was withheld.

Most drastically of all, plans to replace the king were thrown into action. The barons wrote to Louis the Lion, the twenty-seven-year-old son of Philip Augustus, inviting him to come to England, join the war and take the crown for himself. 'This was folly,' wrote William Marshal, Earl of Pembroke, with the benefit of hindsight.[2] But his view was not universally shared. Since Edward the Confessor's day, the English crown had been seized by force on four occasions by princes who were in blood and worldly outlook essentially

OPPOSITE
An illustrated detail from Matthew Paris's major historical work, *Chronica Majora* (1250s). It shows Prince Louis 'the Lion', heir to the French crown, arriving in England in 1216 after he was invited by rebellious barons to invade and replace John. In this ambition he was very nearly successful, and only with the defeats at Lincoln and the naval battles of Dover and Sandwich in 1217 was Louis persuaded to accept a large bribe and return home.

King John's carved wooden effigy surmounting his tomb in Worcester Cathedral. In the words of Sellar & Yeatman's *1066 and All That*, the end of John's 'awful reign' in 1216 came about through 'a surfeit of peaches and no cider'. Had he lived and continued to further alienate a dwindling group of loyal barons, then the rebels and Prince Louis of France might have proved strong enough to overturn the Plantagenet monarchy.

French noblemen.* The difference between supporting the young Henry Plantagenet in 1153–4 and Louis of the House of Capet in 1215–16 may not have struck many noblemen as immediately obvious, even though Henry II could claim to be the grandson of Henry I.

Under extreme pressure, John's hold on England began to weaken. Louis was not the only foreign prince to be invited to invade: the barons of Northern England invited Alexander II, King of Scots, to take over control of Northumberland, Westmorland and Cumberland. In Wales, Llywelyn ap Iorwerth was able to process grandly around, capturing English-held castles and styling himself as 'prince'. And by December, there was already an advance party of French knights in London. John was now battling against three foreign princes, a massive and highly disaffected swathe of his own aristocracy and – as it would transpire – time itself.

Since it was the North that had caused John the bulk of his problems it was here that he first went, marching his men towards the perpetually besieged borderlands town of Berwick, which he took in the first days of 1216 and then burned for good measure. According to the prejudiced but well-informed chronicler Roger of Wendover, John's campaign in the North was calculated to cause maximum terror and remind his subjects that he was, despite everything, still their king. John burned villages and houses, and allowed his mercenaries to rape, murder and steal more or less as they chose. Thirsty as ever for money, he forced men to pay for their own freedom (and that of their families) from the advancing wall of slaughter. He was, said the chronicler Walter of Coventry, 'on the warpath'.[3]

After a successful campaign against the Scots, John turned towards the South-East of England. For several months his brutalizing campaign was

---

*   These occasions were: William the Conqueror in 1066; Henry I's lightning coup against his brother Robert Curthose in 1100; Stephen's seizure of the crown in 1135, which began the Anarchy; and Henry II's deal to inherit the crown in 1154, extracted by military means the previous year.

successful. He swung through Lincoln and Fotheringay before heading into East Anglia, down to Essex and then west towards Oxford. As he went, resistance melted, and castles were turned over to him merely at the sight of his army. By March 1216 even hardline Northerners such as Eustace de Vesci had come to contemplate making peace once more. But peace did not come. In April rumours from France suggested that Louis was about to set sail from Calais. John fortified the Kentish coast and frantically sent a fleet across the Channel, which tried, unsuccessfully, to blockade Louis in port. It was not enough. The French prince landed in England at the end of May 1216, marched through Kent and was greeted in London with huge cheers on 2 June. He promised to restore England's old laws and govern justly.

A flood of damaging defections now battered John. A new papal legate, Guala Bicchieri, had arrived in England to fortify John's cause. But this did not stop several previously loyal barons – including John's own half-brother William Longspée, Earl of Salisbury – from abandoning the king. Over the summer, Louis's troops pushed John out of the South-East once more. In the North, the Scots piled back across the border. Castles held for the king hunkered down to endure long sieges. The country was split between two rival kings. A long and attritional war, similar in character if not cause to the Anarchy, seemed to have begun.

In October 1216, however, the war took an unexpected, but merciful turn. Despite a string of military successes in the early autumn, John had been disappointed to learn that Innocent III had died. He had also received word from Dover that the castle there – one of his vital strongholds against Louis's assault – could not hold out against the French for much longer. Then, while staying at Lynn in Norfolk, John fell violently ill with dysentery. He tried to push through it, but he was very unwell. On 12 October, the sickening king marched his troops north across the River Wellstream, where it ran into the Wash. He, or someone advising him, had not considered the peculiar territorial conditions of the land in the area. The tide was not out far enough and quicksands swallowed up much of the king's baggage train,

along with several of his horses and some of his men. The royal treasure, including John's coronation regalia, was contained in the baggage train and was never seen again.[*]

John escaped, but he was now both sick and furious. He lodged a night at Swineshead Abbey in Lincolnshire, where he was supposedly treated to a feast of ripe peaches and new cider. If these were meant to ease his dysentery, they had quite the opposite effect. His court travelled on, but by 16 October John was in such desperate agony that he had to be carried on a stretcher. He reached Newark and died on the evening of 18 October, after being persuaded – reluctantly – to forgive his enemies.

John's dying wish was that his son Henry, then nine years old, should be his successor. He could scarcely have bequeathed any more troubles on the boy.

---

[*]   The loss of John's baggage train, including the crown jewels, very quickly became a farcical and defining image of the end of John's reign. Ralph of Coggeshall described it briefly and implied that it was a hiccup on John's travels from East Anglia to the Midlands (Stevenson, *Radulphi de Coggeshall Chronicon Anglicanum,* pp. 183–4). When Roger of Wendover came to write up the event in later years, he described it as a major disaster.

10

AFTERLIFE OF THE CHARTER

1215–2015

T he boy king, Henry III, was crowned on 28 October at Gloucester Abbey, with a small corps of long-suffering loyalists including William Marshal and papal legate Guala Bicchieri alongside him. Prince Louis's forces still overran London and the South-East and it was far from clear that the nine-year old Henry would ever recover the formidable royal rule that had been enjoyed by his Plantagenet father, uncle and grandfather. Thus, besides the immediate military necessity of continuing the war against the rebels and the invaders, it was also now vital that the men around Henry offered their enemies some grounds for reconciliation – some gesture that allowed them to believe that with King John dead and buried (his tomb was erected in Worcester Cathedral), the greatest obstacle to peace had been removed. Letters went out to barons offering recompense and restitution to any who would come over to the new king's side. And Magna Carta was reissued for the first time on 12 November 1216.

The effects of this new Magna Carta were not immediate. The war dragged on into 1217, heaping further misery on both sides: William Marshal's biographer reports having seen a hundred Frenchmen lying slain on the ground between Winchester and Romsey, with hungry dogs ripping the flesh from their bones.[1] Eventually, however, the resolve and resources of the French began to pall. Louis left England to attend to business across the Channel for eight weeks in the early spring, and although he came back, during his absence there was a trickle of defections from the rebel camp. Chronicler Roger of Wendover believed that for many of the rebels, the only difficulty in switching sides was the shame of being thought a turncoat.[2]

Yet for all the flagging enthusiasm of the opposition and the growing confidence of the men around Henry, it was several months before a decisive moment was reached in the war. This came at the Battle of Lincoln, on 20 May 1217, when a powerful and impressively armed force led by William Marshal descended on the castle and city, routing the rebels who were camped there and capturing a large number of their leaders. It was a crushing defeat for Louis, from which his cause would never recover. In August

1217, Hubert de Burgh destroyed a French fleet off the Kentish coast at the Battle of Sandwich, and almost immediately a downcast Louis sought terms on which he could depart England without losing too much face. Peace was made in the Treaty of Lambeth on 20 September, and Louis departed the country with a massive bribe of 10,000 marks (a quarter of England's royal annual revenue) to salve his wounded pride. Once he was gone, the business of restoring some normality to government after two years of exhausting civil war began. Magna Carta was once again reissued. This time it was accompanied by a new grant: the Charter of the Forest.

The 1216 and 1217 reissues of Magna Carta contained some important variations from the text of the original made at Runnymede. Strongly worded statements on foreign ministers, which had featured in 1215, were quietly dropped, since many of the most competent men who surrounded Henry III in his minority were themselves of alien birth. The clauses regulating purveyance were redrawn, and there were substantial tweaks made to provisions for widows' rights and the procedures for recovering debts, both to the Crown and to Jewish moneylenders. A clause was introduced in 1217 ordering the destruction of castles that had been erected during the war. New restrictions limited the frequency with which sheriffs could hold their courts. The commitment to investigate historical abuses dating back to Henry II and Richard I's reigns disappeared, although the Charter of the Forest introduced a huge raft of new legislation dealing specifically with woodland law, which promised specifically to return the limits of royal forest land to those that had been in existence in 1154.

And it was from 1217 that Magna Carta earned its famous name – in order to differentiate it from the Charter of the Forest.

It is telling that both the 1216 and 1217 reissues of Magna Carta were presented without the 'security clause'. The question of how to restrain a king out of control would remain alive for the duration of the Middle Ages and beyond, but in 1216 and 1217 it was shelved. Partly this was because its openly bellicose methods had justified civil war instead of promoting peace.

OPPOSITE
Simon de Montfort (*c.*1208–65), Earl of Leicester, one of four local luminaries adorning Leicester's Haymarket Clock Tower, which was built in 1868. This powerful nobleman played a notable role in Magna Carta's evolution during the thirteenth century. The charter was reissued in 1265 under his direction, as he led the opposition to John's son, Henry III. Its association with the English parliamentary tradition dates from this period.

More important, however, was the fact that in just two years Magna Carta had shifted in purpose. Although reissued on both occasions from the jaws of civil war, Magna Carta was no longer primarily a peace treaty imposed by the king's enemies. It was an offering by the king's friends, designed to demonstrate voluntarily the commitment of the new regime to govern by principles on which the whole realm could agree. Magna Carta had mutated from a text of compromise into an assurance of good faith. As it was copied out by clerks and distributed to the shires of England to be read aloud in the sheriffs' courts, the charter had taken on a new purpose.

It did not end there. For the rest of Henry's reign – indeed, for the rest of the thirteenth century – Magna Carta would be reconfirmed and reissued at moments of political instability or crisis. In 1225 Henry III turned eighteen and another, revamped version of the charter was published, given by the king – according to the preamble – 'of our own spontaneous goodwill' (*spontanea et bona voluntate nostra*).[3] This was slightly disingenuous. As Clause 37 of the 1225 edition of Magna Carta made clear, the charters were in fact reissued as one side of a political bargain. The king promised to observe and uphold the customs of the realm, and in return 'all of our realm have given us a fifteenth part of all their movables'. In other words, the king swapped a concession of liberties for tax revenue. This would become an enduring practice. During the course of the thirteenth and fourteenth centuries the English constitution would become anchored by the principle that the king exercised his right to tax his subjects only if he agreed to remedy and reform government. Here, in the 1225 edition of Magna Carta, that idea was made explicit for the first time.

Further reissues followed. In January 1237 both charters were again confirmed in binding and perpetual form, protected by a third 'small charter', whose witnesses included a few old men who had been at Runnymede in 1215. Once again a tax was granted. And by this time something of a myth of Magna Carta had started to grow. The charter was widely circulated with each revision and reissue. Magna Carta was referred to frequently in legal

cases, barons began to offer charters of liberties to their own tenants, which were clearly modelled on the form and content of Magna Carta, and the charter was still protected explicitly by the Church. English parish churches were the venues for readings of Magna Carta in the vernacular. Excommunication was pronounced as the penalty for disobedience in both 1225 and 1237; on 13 May 1253 a confirmation of the charters took place in Westminster Abbey, in which the Archbishop of Canterbury and thirteen bishops passed the familiar sentence of excommunication on those who ignored Magna Carta's provisions. (The saints called upon to observe the sentence included Edward the Confessor and Thomas Becket, both of whom had played their own small roles in the history of opposition to John and his Plantagenet relatives.) When the sentence was passed, the bishops all threw down the lit candles they had been holding and said together: 'Thus are extinguished and reek in Hell all those who attack this sentence.' The king promised to guard Magna Carta in all its terms, which he declared was his duty as a man, a Christian, a knight and an anointed king.

In the century that followed John's promulgation of the charter at Runnymede, the collapse into civil war and the king's death, Magna Carta was probably copied out, in its various editions, more than a thousand times. There remain in existence more than a hundred medieval copies, ranging from those official exemplifications of Magna Carta 1215, held in London, Salisbury and Lincoln, to privately made copies held in abbeys and archives. One of the latter is the elegantly scripted copy that exists among the records of Cerne Abbey in Dorset – a hybrid of the 1217 and 1225 editions, with the Charter of the Forest bolted directly on as though it were part of the same treaty.[4] And these were not merely of antiquarian interest. The importance of the charter was clearly and regularly stated. Even where its clauses grew irrelevant and obsolete, much importance was still attached to the idea of Magna Carta as a bargaining chip, particularly in relation to taxation.

In 1242, at one of the earliest recorded parliaments in English history, Henry III requested financial aid from the realm for a military expedition to

France. He was refused, on the grounds that previous grants of taxation had not resulted in good governance, 'because the king had never, after the granting of the thirtieth [i.e. his requested tax], abided by his charter of liberties, nay had since then oppressed [his subjects] more than usual'.[5] When Henry and his eldest son Edward found themselves embroiled in a long war against Simon de Montfort, Earl of Leicester, during the 1250s and 1260s, Magna Carta was again at the heart of the political wrangling. When de Montfort was at the peak of his powers during the first half of 1265 he not only forced Henry and Edward to swear an oath to obey his own constitution, which de Montfort had established the previous year, but also required the king to reconfirm Magna Carta and the Charter of the Forest. In a sense this took the charter back to its original state – the weapon of a radical rebellious faction in English politics seeking to extract promises from a king by intimidation. But de Montfort's insistence on reconfirming the charters in 1265 was also an illustration of just how symbolically potent the mere name of Magna Carta had become for anyone seeking to put their mark on English government. De Montfort sought legitimacy. He found it by wearing the badge of Magna Carta.[6]

Henry III confirmed, or reissued, Magna Carta on average about once every five years during his reign – and increasingly the charter was promulgated in French and English as well as the Latin in which it had first been written. It was known in Normandy, where it became a model for charters of liberties negotiated there. By Henry's death in 1272, Magna Carta had become a political commonplace, whose significance, if not its precise detail, was etched deep into the minds of Englishmen of almost every literate rank. But the final, and in some ways definitive, version of the charter was produced not under Henry III but during the reign of Edward I (1272–1307).

The reign of this tall, imposing, warmongering king was – although broadly more successful than that of his father and grandfather – still troubled by moments of crisis. The worst came in 1297, when the crippling costs of Edward's wars of conquest (in Wales and Scotland) and resistance (in

Gascony) were rejected by a coalition of barons and bishops, who revolted *en masse* against his heavy-handed rule and relentless financial demands. The compromise that was thrashed out included the *Confirmatio cartarum* (Confirmation of the Charters) of 10 October 1297, by which Magna Carta and the Charter of the Forest were reissued once more, accompanied by other concessions and guarantees of good government. Not all of these would be kept by the king or his descendants – in fact, the history of Magna Carta is largely the history of kings failing to stick to its terms. All the same, by the end of the thirteenth century a peace treaty that had lasted just a few weeks more than eight decades had become, in many ways, the founding stone of the whole system of English law and government.

Edward reissued Magna Carta and the Charter of the Forest for one final time in 1300. Subsequent medieval kings confirmed the charters' terms many times over, but Magna Carta was never again to be copied out and distributed in the same formal fashion as had first occurred in June 1215. Nevertheless, it was appealed to dozens of times in parliamentary petitions and private legislation. It also gave a model for the baronial opposition movements that sprang up during the reigns of Edward II (1307–27) and Richard II (1377–99), both of which attempted to restrain the king by drawing up ordinances and contracts that restricted his behaviour and attempted to force him to rule by co-operation with his leading subjects. Inevitably, time stripped Magna Carta of legal relevance. But its influence – and its legend – survived.

*

By the sixteenth century, Magna Carta was a legal antique. Parliaments still made occasional use of it: in 1497, for example, a Parliament of Henry VII passed an Act which aimed 'to prevent the great deceptions involving weights and measures practised for a long time within this his realm contrary to the statute of Magna Carta and other statutes'.[7] And the charter was preserved

OPPOSITE
The great lawyer Sir Edward
Coke (1552–1634) in his role
as Recorder of London, as
painted by Gilbert Jackson in
1615. A thorn in the side of both
James I and Charles I, Coke
was almost single-handedly
responsible for the 'rediscovery'
of Magna Carta during the
years preceding the civil wars
in the 1640s. After centuries of
decline, and in an era in which
the Stuart monarchs were
hankering after rule by 'divine
right', Magna Carta was once
again at the heart of politics.

in the wider public memory thanks to the arrival of the printing press: the
first printed edition was issued by Richard Pynson in 1508, and Magna Carta
was subsequently included in a prominent position in legal handbooks and
collections of statute, which reinforced the idea that it was the primal law of
the land.[8] But Magna Carta could scarcely be said to have dominated constitutional discourse as it had in the thirteenth century – not least, perhaps,
because its basic content was so much at odds with the political mood of the
times. King John's submission to the pope in 1214 and the charter's explicit
protection of the rights of the English Church would come to sit rather uneasily with the Tudor Royal Supremacy that was created by Acts of Parliament
in the 1530s. When Shakespeare wrote his history play *King John*, probably in
the mid-1590s, there was no mention in it of a charter whose relevance was
clearly thought to escape the minds of London's theatre-going public. For
more than a century Magna Carta was ignored, if not forgotten.

It was not until the seventeenth century that Magna Carta returned to
real prominence in England and beyond. For this was an age when the basic
relationship between Crown and subjects would once again come under intense examination. First, there were the civil wars that broke out under
Charles I, in large part because the king had determined to govern by autocratic, arbitrary and absolute means, attempting to revive feudal aspects of
the monarchy that had long been abandoned, and using his own will to override English laws and customs. Charles's opponents searched for historical
precedent and parallel through which they could state their case against tyranny – and they alighted upon Magna Carta, a seemingly perfect example of
an out-of-control king from centuries past being brought into line. Thus,
under the Stuarts the great charter designed to restrain the Plantagenets was
reborn. It was taken cheerfully out of its historical context and held up as an
'original' constitution – proof that Charles I was betraying not only his own
people but English history at large.

At this time Magna Carta was championed most fiercely by the lawyer
Sir Edward Coke, who, since the days of James I, had been convinced not

only of this ancient treaty's usefulness as a bulwark against Stuart tyranny, but also of its monumental, totemic importance in the broader landscape of English history. In 1619, while condemning abuses in royal government on the grounds that they contravened clauses of Magna Carta, Coke told the House of Commons that the charter had earned its name 'not for the largeness but for the weight'. [9] He cleaved to the idea that the king had no right to tax his subjects without their consent, and he grounded that belief in the historical struggles that had produced Magna Carta.[10] Coke drafted the Petition of Right, passed by both Houses of Parliament in defiance of Charles I's attempts to collect forced loans and arbitrarily imprison his enemies in 1628: this was a very conscious attempt to bind Charles to certain principles of government in precisely the same way that John had been bound by the barons in 1215. Thereafter, Magna Carta was cited at other moments of tumult and crisis during Charles's reign, including the trials of royal allies the Earl of Strafford (1641) and Archbishop Laud (1645).*

The revival of Magna Carta – or at least, the *idea* of Magna Carta – during these years of chaos and civil war added to the mythical status of the document itself, and as a result it began to occupy a cherished place in the story of the English constitution. The realm emerged from the seventeenth century with a sense of the sequential history of English liberty: a history (later associated with the 'Whig' approach) that began with King John at Runnymede and culminated in the passing of the Bill of Rights in 1689. There was, admittedly, tempting ground for believing this to be so at the time. The Bill of Rights was not just loosely modelled on Magna Carta; it sprang out of an age that offered very obvious historical parallels with the early thirteenth century. In 1215 English rebels had secured a charter of rights

---

* The comparison was not entirely misguided. In many ways Charles I acted and suffered just as John did. He was wilful, obstinate and autocratic. His own misdeeds – which were ample – were compounded by those committed by his predecessors. And in the end, he died during the course of a war largely of his own making against his own people. In that sense it is fitting that Magna Carta was revived during Charles's reign.

and attempted to bring a foreign prince to the throne in place of a tyrant. In 1688–9 English rebels actually succeeded in doing precisely that, albeit in a different order, by chasing the Catholic James II from the realm and inviting James's Protestant son-in-law William of Orange to rule in his place, and then securing a broad-ranging statement of English law and custom that would be revered for generations afterwards.

Yet it was not only in England that Magna Carta was to have a profound influence on constitutional development. The second way in which the charter bore down upon the seventeenth century was in its adoption as the basis for the emerging constitutions of the New World. The principles of founding charters had been taken across the Atlantic with the first English colonists, where communities of settlers up and down the Eastern seaboard, from Massachusetts to Georgia, established their governments from the outset according to ideas that they – following Coke – thought had originated in Magna Carta. The colonists saw themselves as English freemen, whose rights were to be afforded precisely the same protection as those in the old country.

In the eighteenth century, this attitude would become a matter of literally world-changing importance. No tax without consent; no imprisonment without due process. These were the issues that lay beneath the declaration and achievement of independence as the American colonies wrenched themselves free from British rule. Magna Carta had been published in the colonies as early as 1687, and just under a century later, as revolution swept through North America, it was to Magna Carta that men turned once again for their inspiration. In October 1774 the delegates to the first Continental Congress of the thirteen discontented colonies explicitly justified their gathering to express grievances by claiming that the colonies were acting simply 'as Englishmen, their ancestors in like cases have usually done'.[11]

When independence had been won, and the newly formed United States of America was busily willing itself into constitutional existence, Magna Carta was again a model. The American Bill of Rights – ratified in

1791 and consisting of the first ten of James Madison's list of constitutional amendments designed to limit the powers of state over citizen – echoes Magna Carta in several places. The Fifth Amendment states that no person should be 'deprived of life, liberty, or property, without due process of law; nor shall private property be taken for public use, without just compensation'. Compare the first half of this with Clause 39 of Magna Carta in 1215: 'No free man is to be arrested, or imprisoned, or disseized, or outlawed, or exiled, or in any other way ruined, nor will we go or send against him, except by the legal judgment of his peers or by the law of the land.' Then compare the second half with Clause 30: 'No sheriff or bailiff of ours, or anyone else may take any free man's horses or carts for transporting things, except with the free man's agreement.' The similarities are striking. So too with the Sixth Amendment of the American document: 'In all criminal prosecutions, the accused shall enjoy the right to a speedy and public trial, by an impartial jury.' What is this if not a reformulation of Clause 40 of Magna Carta 1215 – 'To no one will we sell, to no one will we deny or delay, right or justice'? It is perhaps no surprise that since the earliest years of the United States' existence, its citizens have looked upon Magna Carta with an almost Cokean enthusiasm, which was marked in 1957 by the erection of the only permanent monument to Magna Carta at Runnymede – paid for by the American Bar Association.

By the nineteenth century, therefore, Magna Carta was enshrined in Western political thought as being a document of great and formative importance to modern ideas of freedom. It has remained so ever since – and small parts of the charter can still be found embedded in the constitutions of nations connected with the former British Empire, from Canada to Australia (where a 1297 edition of the charter is on display in Parliament House in Canberra) and New Zealand. Original editions of the charter are highly prized and extremely valuable: during the Second World War the Lincoln copy of Magna Carta 1215 was kept safe in Fort Knox; in December 2007 a copy of Magna Carta 1297, complete with the seal of Edward I, was

THE PATRIOTIC AMERICAN FARMER.
J-N D-K-NS——N Esqr BARRISTER at LAW:
Who with Attic Eloquence and Roman Spirit hath Asserted,
The Liberties of the BRITISH Colonies in America.

Tis nobly done, to Stem Taxations Rage,
And raise, the thoughts of a degen'rate Age,
For Happiness, and Joy, from Freedom Spring,
But Life in Bondage, is a worthless Thing.

Printed for & Sold by R. Bell. Bookseller

bought at auction in New York for an astonishing $21.3 million.

It is true that the majority of Magna Carta's clauses and the circumstances of its creation have long ceased to be politically or legally important, or have been superseded by more recent legislation. Certainly, those clauses that were most important to the handful of English barons who rebelled against King John in 1215 have no bearing at all on life in the twenty-first century. We no longer concern ourselves with feudal dues, or forest laws, or the niceties of levying scutage; and even the grander, catch-all phrases concerning life and liberty have been superseded in English and Scottish law by newer legislation, including the European Human Rights Act.

All the same, a very small number of the charter's most sweeping phrases continue to exert influence. It is still striking to see, when we look at the European Human Rights Act or the United Nations' Universal Declaration of Human Rights, how closely the language of Magna Carta continues to inform our basic legal protections. Here is Article 5 of the European Human Rights Act: 'No one shall be deprived of his liberty save … in accordance with a procedure prescribed by law.' And here is Article 9 of the Universal Declaration of Human Rights, a document that was described at the time of its conception by its champion, Eleanor Roosevelt, as 'the international Magna Carta for all men everywhere': 'No one shall be subjected to arbitrary arrest, detention or exile.' Once again, these are echoes of the famous Clause 39 of Magna Carta 1215. It is not only impossible, but probably fatuous, to imagine that the men who stood in Runnymede in June 1215 imagined that the text they were thrashing out might, in 800 years time, be employed in the defence of the rights of the poorest and meanest citizens in countries in every corner of the world. But that is the way it turned out.

*

One of the great paradoxes of Magna Carta is the fact that the less relevant most of the document's words become to modern life, the greater the rever-

ence that attaches to its name. 'Magna Carta' is today used as a byword for all types of aspiration to freedom, liberty and (quite erroneously) democracy. When Nelson Mandela made the case for his commitment to democratic ideals during his Rivonia Trial in 1964, he told the court: 'The Magna Carta, the Petition of Rights, and the Bill of Rights are documents which are held in veneration by democrats throughout the world.'[12] Mandela's cause was noble, but in truth the link between Magna Carta and democracy is really no more than assumed and associative. No clause of the charter mentions, or was intended to promote, anything that we would today consider 'democratic'; indeed, the idea of democracy was alien and would quite possibly have been offensive to the wealthy, oligarchical and largely self-interested barons who opposed King John in 1215.

Nevertheless, men and women all over the world continue to venerate Magna Carta as a founding text of Western liberal democracy, not always with completely convincing results. In 2014, for example, Prime Minister David Cameron promised, in a speech, to make every schoolchild in the United Kingdom study Magna Carta, saying that 'the remaining copies of that charter may have faded, but its principles shine as brightly as ever, and they paved the way for the democracy, the equality, the respect and the laws that make Britain'.[13] In fact, precisely the opposite is true: many of the remaining copies of the charter are in good condition, while most of their principles are now obsolete, and the clauses have nothing to do with democracy, equality or respect.* But this sort of political platitude is commonplace, and it speaks to the myth of Magna Carta that has developed during the last 800 years. At times that myth can have great political potency: Magna Carta's ancient proclamations against detention without trial were instrumental, in

---

* David Cameron would have been better to follow one of his predecessors as prime minister, Winston Churchill, who wrote that Magna Carta was 'the foundation of principles and systems of government of which neither King John nor his nobles dreamed'.

2008, in defeating the Labour government's Counter-Terrorism Bill, which sought to extend the period for which a person could be imprisoned without charges from 28 to 42 days. At other times, it is used in ways that are rather confused.

This confusion tends to be greatest when Magna Carta is invoked for causes besides the more general ideals of liberal democracy or freedom from tyranny. A 'Magna Carta for the Web' is regularly called for now, to challenge both official (and often covert) monitoring and surveillance of online communications and also the rising power of supra-national organizations – Google, Facebook, Apple, and so on – which are thought to be exercising new and unchecked control over private data, freedom of information and personal reputations.[14] There have been calls in recent years for a Magna Carta for disabled people, for medical banking, for American coal miners and for Filipino call-centre workers.[15] Most amusingly, in 2013 Magna Carta even found its way into mainstream popular culture in the title of one of Jay-Z's hip-hop albums, *Magna Carta Holy Grail*, which sold more than 2 million copies in the United States during the months following its release. Quite what the phrase 'Magna Carta Holy Grail' is supposed to suggest remains obscure – perhaps the artist's desire to rewrite the rules of commercial activity in the music industry. But look past the bathos and we can reflect that it is extraordinary that the phrase 'Magna Carta' has gained such popular currency across the world that it can be co-opted with apparent seriousness into the posturing and sloganeering of mainstream American pop music.

This, then, is where we stand. The second decade of the twenty-first century, accompanied by loud and vigorous discussion, marks the 800th anniversary of an agreement that was born out of two generations of opposition to the excesses of early Plantagenet government during the late twelfth and early thirteenth centuries; this deal, and the parchment on which it was written, came to define nearly a hundred years of political conflict between English kings and their noblemen, and has since passed into the realm of

myth and legend, its name called on in support of all manner of movements in which authority is challenged or restrained by the people.

As time goes by, Magna Carta's name will undoubtedly continue to be hitched to causes both noble and absurd. One thing, however, is certain: the fame and the symbolic importance of this hard-born charter is as great now as at any time in its history. Few other documents can claim such revered status, and few will again. Certainly this would have come as a surprise to the men who stood at Runnymede in June 1215 and thrashed out an unsatisfactory peace treaty. But it is a fitting testament to their struggle.

APPENDIX I

THE TEXT OF MAGNA CARTA 1215

Johannes Dei gratia rex Angliae, dominus Hiberniae, dux Normanniae Aquitanniae, et comes Andegaviae, archiepiscopis, episcopis, abbatibus, comitibus, baronibus, justiciariis, forestariis, vicecomitibus, praepositis, ministris et omnibus ballivis et fidelibus suis salutem. Sciatis nos intuitu Dei et pro salute animae nostrae et omnium antecessorum et haredum nostrorum, ad honorem Dei et exaltationem sanctae ecclesiae, et emendationem regni nostri, per consilium venerabilium patrum nostrorum, Stephani Cantuariensis archiepiscopi totius Angliae primatis et sanctae Romanae ecclesiae cardinalis, Henrici Dublinensis archiepiscopi, Willelmi Londoniensis, Petri Wintoniensis, Joscelini Bathoniensis et Glastoniensis, Hugoni Lincolniensis, Walteri Wygornensis, Willelmi Coventrensis, et Benedicti Roffensis episcoporum; magistri Pandulfi domini papae subdiaconi et familiaris, fratris Eymerici magistri militiae Templi in Anglia; et nobilium virorum Willelmi Mariscalli comitis Penbrociae, Willelmi comitis Saresberiae, Willelmi comitis Warenniae, Willelmi comitis Arundelliae, Alani de Galweya constabularii Scottiae, Warini filii Geroldi, Petri filii Hereberti, Huberti de Burgo senescalli Pictaviae, Hugonis de Nevilla, Mathei filii Hereberti, Thomae Basset, Alani Basset, Philippo de Albiniaco, Roberti de Roppel, Johannis Mariscalli, Johannis filii Hugonis et aliorum fidelium nostrorum:

John, by the grace of God King of England, Lord of Ireland, Duke of Normandy and Aquitaine, Count of Anjou, to his archbishops, bishops, abbots, earls, barons, justices, foresters, sheriffs, reeves, officers and all his bailiffs and faithful subjects, greetings. Know that, for the sake of God and for the salvation of our soul and the souls of all our ancestors and heirs, to the honour of God and the exaltation of the holy Church, and for the reform of our realm, by the advice of our venerable fathers Stephen, Archbishop of Canterbury, Primate of All England and Cardinal of the Holy Roman Church; Henry, Archbishop of Dublin; William, Bishop of London; Peter, Bishop of Winchester; Jocelin, Bishop of Bath and Glastonbury; Hugh, Bishop of Lincoln; Walter, Bishop of Worcester; William, Bishop of Coventry; and Benedict, Bishop of Rochester; Master Pandulf, subdeacon and confidant of the lord pope; Brother Aymeric, Master of the Knights Templar in England; and the noble men William Marshal, Earl of Pembroke; William, Earl of Salisbury; William, Earl Warenne; William, Earl of Arundel; Alan of Galloway, Constable of Scotland; Warin FitzGerald; Peter FitzHerbert; Hubert de Burgh, Seneschal of Poitou; Hugh de Neville; Matthew FitzHerbert; Thomas Basset; Alan Basset; Philip d'Aubigny; Robert de Roppel; John Marshal; John FitzHugh and other of our faithful subjects:

1 *In primis concessisse Deo et hac praesenti carta nostra confirmasse, pro nobis et haeredibus nostris in perpetuum, quod Anglicana ecclesia libera sit, et habeat jura sua integra, et libertates suas illaesas; et ita volumus observari; quod apparet ex eo quod libertatem electionum, quae maxima et magis necessaria reputatur ecclesiae Anglicanae, mera et spontanea voluntate, ante discordiam inter nos et barones nostros motam, concessimus et carta nostra confirmavimus, et eam obtinuimus a domino papa Innocentio tertio confirmari; quam et nos observabimus et ab haeredibus nostris in perpetuum bona fide volumus observari. Concessimus etiam omnibus liberis hominibus regni nostri, pro nobis et haeredibus nostris in perpetuum, omnes libertates subscriptas, habendas et tenendas, eis et haeredibus suis, de nobis et haeredibus nostris.*

2 *Si quis comitum vel baronum nostrorum, sive aliorum tenentium de nobis in capite per servitium militare, mortuus fuerit, et cum decesserit haeres suus plenae aetatis fuerit et relevium debeat, habeat haereditatem suam per antiquum relevium; scilicet haeres vel haeredes comitis de baronia comitis integra per centum libras; haeres vel haeredes baronis de baronia integra per centum libras; haeres vel haeredes militis de feodo militis integro per centum solidos ad plus; et qui minus debuerit minus det secundum antiquam consuetudinem feodorum.*

1 Firstly, we have granted to God and confirmed by this, our present charter, for us and our heirs in perpetuity, that the English Church shall be free, and shall have its rights in full and its liberties intact; and we wish this to be thus observed, which is clear from the fact that, before the discord with our barons began, we granted and confirmed by our charter free elections, which are considered to be of the utmost importance and necessity to the English Church, and we obtained confirmation of this from our lord Pope Innocent III; which we shall observe and which we wish our heirs to observe in good faith in perpetuity. We have also granted to all the free men of our realm, for ourselves and our heirs in perpetuity, all the liberties written below, for them and their heirs to have and to hold of us and our heirs.

2 If any of our earls or barons, or others holding in chief* of us by knight service, dies, and at his death his heir is of full age and owes relief, he shall have his inheritance by paying the ancient relief: that is, for the heir or heirs of an earl, £100 for the whole earl's barony; for the heir or heirs of a baron, £100 for the whole barony; for the heir or heirs of a knight, 100 marks at most for the whole knight's fee; and anyone who owes less gives less, according to the ancient custom of fees.

---

* 'Holding in chief' – i.e. as tenant-in-chief, holding land directly from the Crown.

3 *Si autem haeres alicujus talium fuerit infra aetatem et fuerit in custodia, cum ad aetatem pervenerit, habeat haereditatem suam sine relevio et sine fine.*

3 If, on the other hand, the heir of any such person has been underage and has been in wardship, when he comes of age he is to have his inheritance without paying relief and without a fine.

4 *Custos terrae hujusmodi haeredis qui infra aetatem fuerit, non capiat de terra haeredis nisi rationabiles exitus, et rationabiles consuetudines, et rationabilia servitia, et hoc sine destructione et vasto hominum vel rerum; et si nos commiserimus custodiam alicujus talis terrae vicecomiti vel alicui alii qui de exitibus illius nobis respondere debeat, et ille destructionem de custodia fecerit vel vastum, nos ab illo capiemus emendam, et terra committatur duobus legalibus et discretis hominibus de feodo illo, qui de exitibus respondeant nobis vel ei cui eos assignaverimus; et si dederimus vel vendiderimus alicui custodiam alicujus talis terrae, et ille destructionem inde fecerit vel vastum, amittat ipsam custodiam, et tradatur duobus legalibus et discretis hominibus de feodo illo qui similiter nobis respondeant sicut praedictum est.*

4 The guardian of the land of such an heir who is underage, shall not take from the heir's land any more than reasonable revenues, reasonable customs and reasonable services, and this shall be done without the destruction or waste of men or goods; and if we have committed the wardship of any such land to a sheriff or anyone else who answers to us for its revenues, and he destroys or wastes the lands, we will take amends from him, and the land shall be committed to two law-abiding and discreet men of the fee,* who will answer to us or the person we have assigned them, and if we give or sell the wardship of any such land to anyone, and he destroys or wastes it, he shall lose the wardship, and it shall be handed over to two law-abiding and discreet men of the fee who shall answer to us as previously said.

---

*   'Men of the fee' – men connected to the land in question.

5 *Custos autem, quamdiu custodiam terrae habuerit, sustentet domos, parcos, vivaria, stagna, molendina, et cetera ad terram illam pertinentia, de exitibus terrae ejusdem; et reddat haeredi, cum ad plenam aetatem pervenerit, terram suam totam instauratam de carrucis et wainnagiis, secumdum quod tempus wainnagii exiget et exitus terrae rationabiliter poterunt sustinere.*

5 Moreover, so long as the guardian has wardship of the land, he shall maintain out of the revenues of the land the buildings, parks, fishponds, pools, mills, and other things pertaining to the land; and when the heir comes of age he shall restore to him all his land stocked with ploughs and growing crops, such as the agricultural season requires and the revenues of the land can reasonably sustain.

6 *Haeredes maritentur absque disparagatione, ita tamen quod, antequam contrahatur matrimonium, ostendatur propinquis de consanguinitate ipsius haeredis.*

6 Heirs shall be married without disparagement, provided that before a marriage is contracted, the heir's closest relatives are informed.

The global phenomenon of Magna Carta. This is a 1297 copy of Magna Carta, one of four surviving copies, which was bought by Australia's government from an English school in 1952 (price: £12,500). It is now proudly displayed in Parliament House, Canberra. Certain clauses of the 1215 charter – principally 39 and 40 – have been used as the basis for constitutions in countries across the English-speaking world.

7   *Vidua post mortem mariti sui statim et sine difficultate habeat maritagium et haereditatem suam, nec aliquid det pro dote sua, vel pro maritagio suo, vel haereditate sua quam haereditatem maritus suus et ipsa tenuerint die obitus ipsius mariti, et maneat in domo mariti sui per quadraginta dies post mortem ipsius, infra quos assignetur ei dos sua.*

8   *Nulla vidua distringatur ad se maritandum dum voluerit vivere sine marito, ita tamen quod securitatem faciat quod se non maritabit sine assensu nostro, si de nobis tenuerit, vel sine assensu domini sui de quo tenuerit, si de alio tenuerit.*

9   *Nec nos nec ballivi nostri seisiemus terram aliquam nec redditum pro debito aliquo, quamdiu catalla debitoris sufficiunt ad debitum reddendum; nec pleggii ipsius debitoris distringantur quamdiu ipse capitalis debitor sufficit ad solutionem debiti; et si capitalis debitor defecerit in solutione debiti, non habens unde solvat, pleggii respondeant de debito; et, si voluerint, habeant terras et redditus debitoris donec sit eis satisfactum de debito quod ante pro eo solverint, nisi capitalis debitor monstraverit se esse quietum inde versus eosdem pleggios.*

7   After the death of her husband a widow shall have her marriage portion and inheritance straightaway and without difficulty, nor shall she pay anything for her dower, her marriage portion or her inheritance which she and her husband held on the day of his death. She may remain in her marital home for forty days after his death, during which period her dower will be assigned to her.

8   No widow shall be forced to marry for as long as she wishes to live without a husband, provided that she gives security that she will not marry without our consent, if she holds of us, or without the consent of her lord of whom she holds, if she holds of someone else.

9   Neither we nor our bailiffs will seize any land or any rent for any debt, so long as the debtor's chattels are sufficient to pay the debt; nor are the pledges of the debtor to be distrained so long as the principal debtor has enough to pay the debt. And if the principal debtor defaults on the debt, not having the means to pay it, the pledges are to answer for it. And if they wish, they may have the debtor's lands and rents until they have had satisfaction for the debt they have settled for him, unless the principal debtor demonstrates that he is quit with regard to the pledges.

10 Si quis mutuo ceperit aliquid a Judaeis, plus vel minus, et moriatur antequam debitum illud solvatur, debitum non usuret quamdiu haeres fuerit infra aetatem, de quocumque teneat; et si debitum illud inciderit in manus nostras, nos non capiemus nisi catallum contentum in carta.

10 If anyone has taken any sort of loan from the Jews, great or small, and dies before the debt is settled, the debt shall not carry interest for as long as the heir is underage, whoever he holds from; and if that debt should fall into our hands, we will take nothing but the principal sum recorded in the charter.

11 Et si quis moriatur, et debitum debeat Judaeis, uxor ejus habeat dotem suam, et nihil reddat de debito illo; et si liberi ipsius defuncti qui fuerint infra aetatem remanserint, provideantur eis necessaria secundum tenementum quod fuerit defuncti, et de residuo solvatur debitum, salvo servitio dominorum; simili modo fiat de debitis quae debentur aliis quam Judaeis.

11 And if anyone should die owing a debt to the Jews, his wife shall have her dower and pay nothing of that debt; and if he leaves surviving children who are underage, their needs are to be provided for according to the holding of the deceased, and the debt shall be paid from what remains, saving the service owed to the lords. Debts owed to others besides the Jews are to be dealt with in the same way.

12 Nullum scutagium vel auxilium ponatur in regno nostro, nisi per commune consilium regni nostri, nisi ad corpus nostrum redimendum, et primogenitum filium nostrum militem faciendum, et ad filiam nostram primogenitam semel maritandam, et ad haec non fiat nisi rationabile auxilium; simili modo fiat de auxiliis de civitate Londoniarum.

12 No scutage or other aid is to be levied in our realm, except by the common counsel of our realm, unless it is to pay for the ransoming of our person, the knighting of our first-born son or the first marriage of our first-born daughter; and for these only a reasonable aid is to be taken. Aids taken from the City of London will be treated in the same way.

13 Et civitas Londoniarum habeat omnes antiquas libertates et liberas consuetudines suas, tam per terras quam per aquas. Praeterea volumus et concedimus quod omnes aliae civitates, et burgi, et villae, et portus, habeant omnes libertates et liberas consuetudines suas.

14 Et ad habendum commune consilium regni de auxilio assidendo aliter quam in tribus casibus praedictis, vel de scutagio assidendo, summoneri faciemus archiepiscopos, episcopos, abbates, comites, et majores barones sigillatim per litteras nostras; et praeterea faciemus summoneri in generali per vicecomites et ballivos nostros, omnes illos qui de nobis tenent in capite ad certum diem, scilicet ad terminum quadraginta dierum ad minus, et ad certum locum; et in omnibus litteris illius summonitionis causam summonitionis exprimemus; et sic facta summonitione negotium ad diem assignatum procedat secundum consilium illorum qui praesentes fuerint, quamvis non omnes summoniti venerint.

15 Nos non concedemus de cetero alicui quod capiat auxilium de liberis hominibus suis, nisi ad corpus suum redimendum, et ad faciendum primogenitum filium suum militem, et ad primogenitam filiam suam semel maritandam, et ad haec non fiat nisi rationabile auxilium.

13 And the City of London shall have all its ancient liberties and free customs both on land and on water. Furthermore we wish and grant that all other cities, boroughs, towns and ports shall have all their liberties and free customs.

14 And for us to have common counsel of the realm for the levying of an aid (other than in the three cases previously mentioned) or for the levying of a scutage, we will have archbishops, bishops, abbots, earls and greater barons summoned individually by our letters; and furthermore we will have a general summons, made by our sheriffs and bailiffs, of all of those who hold from us in chief for a fixed day, at least forty days away, and at a fixed place; and in all our letters we will explain the cause of the summons. And when the summons has thus been made, the business shall proceed on the agreed day according to the counsel of those present, even if not all of those summoned have come.

15 In future we will not grant to anyone that he may take an aid from his free men, except to pay a ransom on his person, or on the knighting of his first-born son, or on the first marriage of his first-born daughter; and for these there is only to be a reasonable aid.

16 *Nullus distringatur ad faciendum majus servitium de feodo militis, nec de alio libero tenemento, quam inde debetur.*

16 No one is to be distrained to do more service for a knight's fee, or for any other free tenement, than is owed for it.

17 *Communia placita non sequantur curiam nostram, sed teneantur in aliquo loco certo.*

17 Common pleas are not to follow our court, but are to be held in some fixed place.

18 *Recognitiones de nova dissaisina, de morte ancestoris, et de ultima praesentatione, non capiantur nisi in suis comitatibus et hoc modo; nos, vel si extra regnum fuerimus capitalis justiciarius noster, mittemus duos justiciarios per unumquemque comitatum per quatuor vices in anno, qui, cum quatuor militibus cujuslibet comitatus electis per comitatum, capiant in comitatu et in die et loco comitatus assisas praedictas.*

18 Recognizances of novel disseizin, mort d'ancestor and darrein presentment* are not to be held except in their proper county court, and in this way: we, or if we are out of the realm our Chief Justiciar,† shall send two justices to each county four times a year, who, with four knights of each county chosen by the county court, shall hold the said assizes in the county court, on the day and in the meeting place of the county court.

19 *Et si in die comitatus assisae praedictae capi non possint, tot milites et libere tenentes remaneant de illis qui interfuerint comitatui die illo, per quos possint judicia sufficienter fieri, secundum quod negotium fuerit majus vel minus.*

19 And if on the day of the county court the said assizes cannot be held, as many knights and free tenants [as are required] out of those who were present in the county court on that day will remain for the sufficient making of judgments, according to whether the business is great or small.

---

* 'Novel disseizin, mort d'ancestor and darrein presentment' – common legal procedures initiated by writs of Chancery, all connected with ownership of property.

† '(Chief) Justiciar' – the principal royal servant in legal and political matters, effectively a chief minister, sometimes regent.

In CONGRESS, July 4, 1776.

The unanimous Declaration of the thirteen united States of America.

20 *Liber homo non amercietur pro parvo delicto, nisi secundum modum delicti; et pro magno delicto amercietur secundum magnitudinem delicti, salvo contenemento suo; et mercator eodem modo, salva mercandisa sua; et villanus eodem modo amercietur salvo wainnagio suo; si inciderint in misericordiam nostram; et nulla praedictarum misericordiarum ponatur, nisi per sacramentum proborum hominum de visneto.*

20 A free man may not be amerced [i.e. fined] for a small offence, except according to the nature of the offence; and for a great offence he shall be amerced according to the magnitude of the offence, saving his livelihood; and a merchant in the same way, saving his merchandise; and a villein shall be amerced in the same way, saving his growing crops, if they fall into our mercy. And none of the said amercements may be made, except upon the oaths of honest men of the neighbourhood.

21 *Comites et barones non amercientur nisi per pares suos, et non nisi secundum modum delicti.*

21 Earls and barons are not to be amerced except by their peers, and only in accordance with the nature of the offence.

The 1823 facsimile of the American Declaration of Independence of 4 July 1776, whereby the thirteen rebellious colonies threw down the gauntlet against what was perceived as the British monarch's attempt to impose an 'absolute Tyranny'. It is perhaps unsurprising that in the United States Magna Carta is considered a precursor to the Declaration. Yet there are more differences than similarities – and while the Declaration spoke in the collected voices of the rebels, who famously signed their names, Magna Carta was ostensibly the king's singular voice, authorized under his seal.

22 *Nullus clericus amercietur de laico tenemento suo, nisi secundum modum aliorum praedictorum, et non secundum quantitatem beneficii sui ecclesiastici.*

22 No clergyman is to be amerced on his lay tenement, except in accordance with the nature of his offence, in the way of others mentioned previously, and not in accordance with the size of his ecclesiastical benefice.

23 *Nec villa nec homo distringatur facere pontes ad riparias, nisi qui ab antiquo et de jure facere debent.*

23 Neither town nor man shall be forced to build bridges over rivers, except those who are obliged to do so by custom and right.

24 *Nullus vicecomes, constabularius, coronatores, vel alii ballivi nostri, teneant placita coronae nostrae.*

24 No sheriff, constable, coroner or other of our bailiffs shall hold the pleas of our crown.

25 *Omnes comitatus, hundredi, wapentakii, et trethingii sint ad antiquas firmas absque ullo incremento, exceptis dominicis maneriis nostris.*

25 All counties, hundreds, wapentakes and ridings* shall be at their ancient farms, without any increment, except for our demesne manors.

———————

*   'Hundreds, wapentakes and ridings' – administrative subdivisions of counties or shires, with their origins in Anglo-Saxon times; 'farms' – fixed sums of money due annually in taxation from an area of land.

26 *Si aliquis tenens de nobis laicum feodum moriatur, et vicecomes vel ballivus noster ostendat litteras nostras patentes de summonitione nostra de debito quod defunctus nobis debuit, liceat vicecomiti vel ballivo nostro attachiare et inbreviare catalla defuncti inventa in laico feodo, ad valentiam illius debiti, per visum legalium hominum, ita tamen quod nihil amoveatur, donec persolvatur nobis debitum quod clarum fuerit, et residuum relinquatur executoribus ad faciendum testamentum defuncti; et, si nihil nobis debeatur ab ipso, omnia catalla cedant defuncto, salvis uxoris ipsius et pueris rationabilibus partibus suis.*

27 *Si aliquis liber homo intestatus decesserit, catalla sua per manus propinquorum parentum et amicorum suorum, per visum ecclesiae distribuantur, salvis unicuique debitis quae defunctus ei debebat.*

28 *Nullus constabularius, vel alius ballivus noster, capiat blada vel alia catalla alicujus, nisi statim inde reddat denarios, aut respectum inde habere possit de voluntate venditoris.*

26 If anyone holding a lay fee of us dies, and our sheriff or bailiff shows our letters patent of a summons for a debt which the deceased owed us, it is to be lawful for our sheriff or bailiff to attach and record the chattels of the deceased found on the lay fee, to the value of the debt, in the view of law-abiding men, so that nothing is to be removed from there, until the clear debt is paid to us, and the residue is to be relinquished by the executors to carry out the will of the deceased; and, if nothing is owed to us by him, all the chattels shall go to the deceased, saving reasonable portions for his wife and children.

27 If any free man dies intestate, his chattels are to be distributed by his closest kinsmen and friends, under the supervision of the Church, saving to everyone the debts that the dead man owed them.

28 No constable, or any of our bailiffs, shall take anyone's corn or any other chattels, unless he immediately pays for them in cash, or else he can agree with the seller to postpone payment.

29 *Nullus constabularius distringat aliquem militem ad dandum denarios pro custodia castri, si facere voluerit custodiam illam in propria persona sua, vel per alium probum hominem, si ipse eam facere non possit propter rationabilem causam; et si nos duxerimus vel miserimus eum in exercitum, erit quietus de custodia, secundum quantitatem temporis quo per nos fuerit in exercitu.*

29 No constable may compel any knight to give money instead of performing castle guard, if he is willing to perform that guard in person, or, if he is for some good reason unable to do it himself, through another reliable man. And if we have led or sent him in the army, he shall be relieved of guard duty, in accordance with the amount of time he spent in our military service.

30 *Nullus vicecomes, vel ballivus noster, vel aliquis alius, capiat equos vel caretas alicujus liberi hominis pro cariagio faciendo, nisi de voluntate ipsius liberi hominis.*

30 No sheriff or bailiff of ours, or anyone else, may take any free man's horses or carts for transporting things, except with the free man's agreement.

31 *Nec nos nec ballivi nostri capiemus alienum boscum ad castra vel alia agenda nostra, nisi per voluntatem ipsius cujus boscus ille fuerit.*

31 Neither we nor our bailiffs may take anyone's timber to a castle or to any other business of ours, except with the agreement of the timber's owner.

32 *Nos non tenebimus terras illorum qui convicti fuerint de felonia, nisi per unum annum et unum diem, et tunc reddantur terrae dominis feodorum.*

32 We will not hold the lands of convicted felons for more than a year and a day, and then the lands will be returned to the lord of the fee.

33 *Omnes kydelli de cetero deponantur penitus de Thamisia, et de Medewaye, et per totam Angliam, nisi per costeram maris.*

33 In future, all fish-weirs will be completely removed from the Thames and the Medway and throughout the whole of England, except on the sea-coast.

34   *Breve quod vocatur Praecipe de cetero non fiat alicui de aliquo tenemento unde liber homo amittere possit curiam suam.*

34   The writ called Praecipe will not, in future, be issued to anyone for any holding in respect of which a free man could lose his court.

35   *Una mensura vini sit per totum regnum nostrum, et una mensura cervisie, et una mensura bladi, scilicet quarterium Londoniense, et una latitudo pannorum tinctorum et russetorum et halbergettorum, scilicet duae ulnae infra listas; de ponderibus autem sit ut de mensuris.*

35   There shall be one measure of wine in the whole of our realm, and one measure of ale, and one measure of corn, namely, the quarter of London, and one width of dyed, russet and haberget cloths, namely two ells within the borders. Let it be the same for weights as it is for measures.

36   *Nihil detur vel capiatur de cetero pro brevi inquisitionis de vita vel membris, sed gratis concedatur et non negetur.*

36   Nothing shall in future be given or taken for the writ of inquisition of life and limb, but it shall be freely given and not refused.

37   *Si aliquis teneat de nobis per feodifirmam, vel per sokagium, vel per burgagium, et de alio terram teneat per servitium militare, nos non habebimus custodiam haeredis nec terrae suae quae est de feodo alterius, occasione illius feodifirmae, vel sokagii, vel burgagii; nec habebimus custodiam illius feodifirmae, vel sokagii, vel burgagii, nisi ipsa feodifirma debeat servitium militare. Nos non habebimus custodiam haeredis vel terrae alicujus, quam tenet de alio per servitium militare, occasione alicujus parvae sergenteriae quam tenet de nobis per servitium reddendi nobis cultellos, sagittas, vel hujusmodi.*

37   If anyone holds of us by fee-farm, socage or burgage*, and holds land of someone else by military service, we will not, by reason of the fee-farm, socage or burgage, have wardship of his heir or of his lands belonging to another man's fee. Nor will we have custody of that fee-farm, socage or burgage, except if the fee-farm, socage or burgage owes military service. We will not have custody of anyone's heir or anyone's lands which he holds of someone else by military service, by virtue of some petty serjeantry by which he holds of us by the service of rendering us knives, or arrows, or suchlike.

---

*   'Fee-farm, socage or burgage' – different forms of feudal tenure (where payments or military services are owed to the king in return for possession of land).

38 *Nullus ballivus ponat de cetero aliquem ad legem simplici loquela sua, sine testibus fidelibus ad hoc inductis.*

38 No bailiff is in future to put anyone to law by his accusation alone, without trustworthy witnesses being brought forward.

39 *Nullus liber homo capiatur, vel imprisonetur, aut dissaisiatur, aut utlagetur, aut exuletur, aut aliquo modo destruatur, nec super eum ibimus, nec super eum mittemus, nisi per legale judicium parium suorum vel per legem terrae.*

39 No free man is to be arrested, or imprisoned, or disseized, or outlawed, or exiled, or in any other way ruined, nor will we go or send against him, except by the legal judgment of his peers or by the law of the land.

40 *Nulli vendemus, nulli negabimus aut differemus, rectum aut justiciam.*

40 To no one will we sell, to no one will we deny or delay, right or justice.

41 *Omnes mercatores habeant salvum et securum exire de Anglia, et venire in Angliam, et morari et ire per Angliam, tam per terram quam per aquam, ad emendum et vendendum sine omnibus malis toltis, per antiquas et rectas consuetudines, praeterquam in tempore gwerrae, et si sint de terra contra nos gwerrina; et si tales inveniantur in terra nostra in principio gwerrae, attachientur sine dampno corporum et rerum, donec sciatur a nobis vel capitali justiciario nostro quomodo mercatores terrae nostrae tractentur, qui tunc invenientur in terra contra nos gwerrina; et si nostri salvi sint ibi, alii salvi sint in terra nostra.*

41 All merchants are to be safe and secure in leaving and coming to England, and in staying and travelling in England, both by land and by water, to buy and sell without any evil tolls, but only by the ancient and rightful customs, save in time of war if they come from an enemy country. And if such are found in our land at the beginning of war, they will be detained without damage to their persons or goods, until it is clear to us or our Chief Justiciar how the merchants of our land are treated in the enemy country; and if ours are safe there, the others shall be safe in our land.

42   *Liceat unicuique de cetero exire de regno nostro, et redire, salvo et secure, per terram et aquam, salva fide nostra, nisi tempore gwerrae per aliquod breve tempus, propter communem utilitatem regni, exceptis imprisonatis et utlagatis secundum legem regni, et gente de terra contra nos gwerrina, et mercatoribus, de quibus fiat sicut praedictum est.*

42   In future it is lawful for anyone, saving his allegiance to us, and except for a short period during time of war, to leave our realm and return, safe and secure by land and water, for the sake of the general good of the realm; except for those imprisoned or outlawed according to the law of the land, and people from the enemy country, and merchants – who shall be treated as previously described.

43   *Si quis tenuerit de aliqua escaeta, sicut de honore Walingeford, Notingeham, Bononiae, Lainkastriae, vel de aliis eskaetis quae sunt in manu nostra et sunt baroniae, et obierit, haeres ejus non det aliud relevium, nec faciat nobis aliud servitium quam faceret baroni si baronia illa esset in manu baronis; et nos eodem modo eam tenebimus quo baro eam tenuit.*

43   If anyone dies who held of any escheat, such as the honours of Wallingford, Nottingham, Boulogne, Lancaster, or of other escheats* which are in our hand and our baronies, his heir will not pay any relief or do us any other service than he would have done to the baron if the barony was in the baron's hand; and we will hold it in the same manner as the baron held it.

44   *Homines qui manent extra forestam non veniant de cetero coram justiciariis nostra de foresta per communes summonitiones, nisi sint in placito, vel pleggii alicujus vel aliquorum, qui attachiati sint pro foresta.*

44   From now on men who reside outside the forest will not come before our justices of the forest on a general summons, unless they are impleaded, or they are pledges for any person or persons who are attached for forest business.

45   *Nos non faciemus justiciarios, constabularios, vicecomites, vel ballivos, nisi de talibus qui sciant legem regni et eam bene velint observare.*

45   We will not appoint justices, constables, sheriffs or bailiffs, other than those who know the law of the realm and intend to keep it well.

---

*   'Escheat' – land that reverted to its lord if the tenant were to die without an heir.

46 *Omnes barones qui fundaverunt abbatias, unde habent cartas regum Angliae, vel antiquam tenuram, habeant earum custodiam cum vacaverint, sicut habere debent.*

46 All barons who have founded abbeys, for which they have charters of the kings of England, or ancient tenure, shall have custody of the abbeys when they are vacant, as they should have.

47 *Omnes forestae quae afforestatae sunt tempore nostro, statim deafforestentur; et ita fiat de ripariis quae per nos tempore nostro positae sunt in defenso.*

47 All forests which have been afforested in our time shall be immediately disafforested, and let the same be done for riverbanks which have been fenced off during our time.

48 *Omnes malae consuetudines, de forestis et warennis, et de forestariis et warennariis, vicecomitibus et eorum ministris, ripariis et earum custodibus, statim inquirantur in quolibet comitatu per duodecim milites juratos de eodem comitatu, qui debent eligi per probos homines ejusdem comitatus, et infra quadraginta dies post inquisitionem factam, penitus, ita quod numquam revocentur, deleantur per eosdem, ita quod nos hoc sciamus prius, vel justiciarius noster, si in Anglia non fuerimus.*

48 All evil customs, of forests and warrens, and of foresters and warreners, sheriffs and their officers, riverbanks and their keepers are immediately to be investigated in each and every county by twelve sworn knights of the same county, who are to be chosen by upright men of their county, and within forty days of the inquiry [the evil customs] are to be entirely abolished, provided that we, or our justiciar if we are not in England, know about it first.

Magna Carta – a multimillion dollar legacy. In 2007 this rarity, one of the four surviving 1297 copies of Magna Carta, came up for sale. It was duly bought by American businessman David Rubenstein for $21.3 million and later loaned to the US National Archives for public display. If the modern understanding of Magna Carta is often at odds with its reality, and its relevance to modern laws and life is questionable, the continued reverence for its historical place in the relations between those who govern and those who are governed endures.

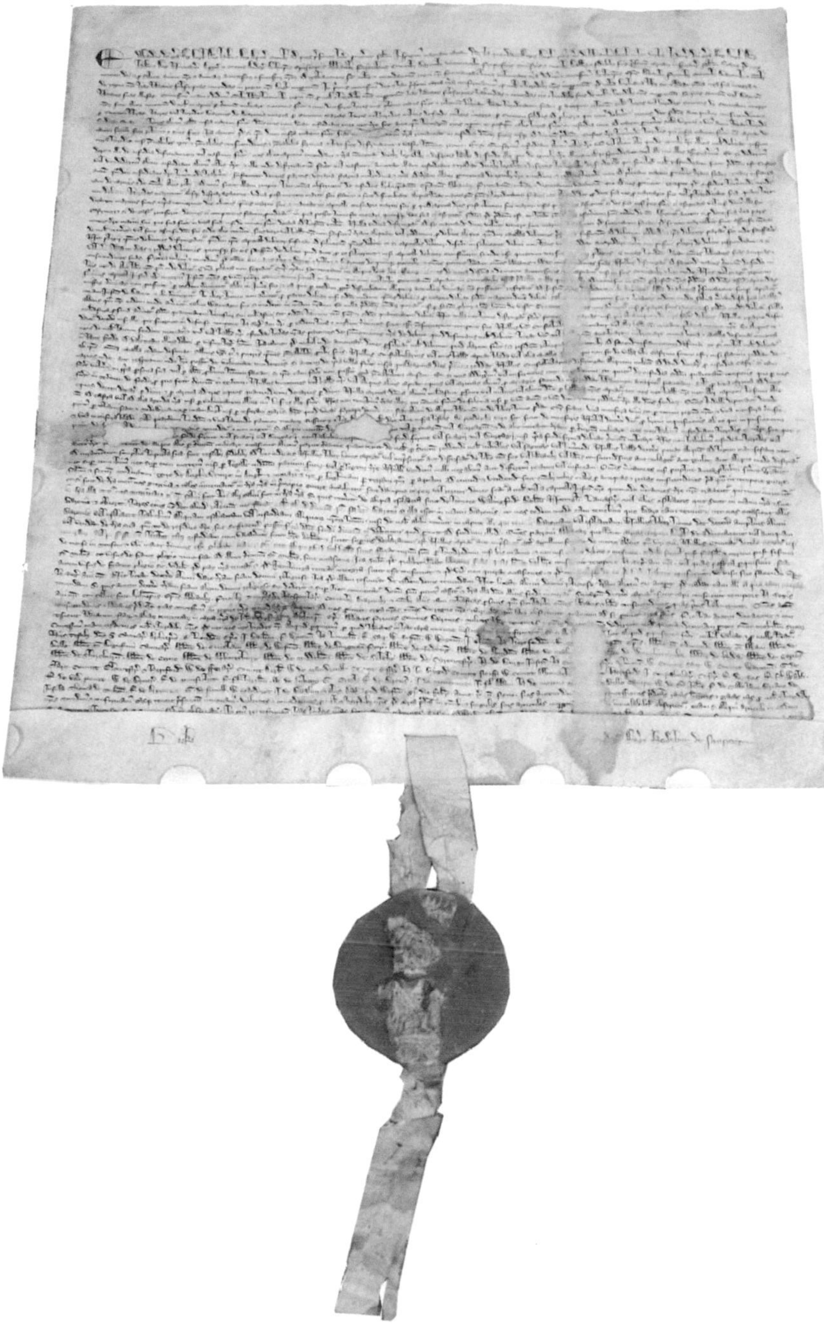

49 *Omnes obsides et cartas statim reddemus quae liberatae fuerunt nobis ab Anglicis in securitatem pacis vel fidelis servitii.*

49 We will immediately restore all hostages and charters that have been given to us by Englishmen as security for peace and faithful service.

50 *Nos amovebimus penitus de balliis parentes Gerardi Athyes, quod de cetero nullam habeant balliam in Anglia: Engelardum de Cygony, Petrum et Gyonem et Andream de Cancellis, Gyonem de Cygony, Galfridum de Martinni et fratres ejus, Philippum Marc et fratres ejus, et Galfridum nepotem ejus, et totam sequelam eorumdem.*

50 We will completely remove from their offices the relations of Gerard d'Athée, so that from now on they shall have no office in England: Engelard de Cigogné, Peter and Guy and Andrew de Chanceaux, Guy de Cigogné, Geoffrey de Martini and his brothers, Philip Mark and his brothers, and his nephew Geoffrey, and all their followers.*

51 *Et statim post pacis reformationem amovebimus de regno omnes alienigenas milites, balistarios, servientes, stipendarios, qui venerint cum equis et armis ad nocumentum regni.*

51 And immediately after the restoration of peace we will remove from the realm all foreign knights, crossbowmen, serjeants and mercenaries, who have come with horses and arms to the detriment of the kingdom.

---

* This group represented the only people to be condemned specifically by name in Magna Carta: the foreign mercenary captain Gerard d'Athée and his relatives had been rewarded for their service to John with high office in England and favour at court.

52 *Si quis fuerit dissaisitus vel elongatus per nos sine legali judicio parium suorum, de terris, castellis, libertatibus, vel jure suo, statim ea ei restituemus; et si contentio super hoc orta fuerit, tunc inde fiat per judicium viginti quinque baronum, de quibus fit mentio inferius in securitate pacis. De omnibus autem illis de quibus aliquis disseisitus fuerit vel elongatus sine legali judicio parium suorum, per Henricum regem patrem nostrum vel per Ricardum regem fratrem nostrum, quae in manu nostra habemus, vel quae alii tenent, quae nos oporteat warantizare, respectum habebimus usque ad communem terminum crucesignatorum, exceptis illis de quibus placitum motum fuit vel inquisitio facta per praeceptum nostrum ante susceptionem crucis nostrae; cum autem redierimus de peregrinatione nostra, vel si forte remanserimus a peregrinatione nostra, statim inde pleman justiciam exhibebimus.*

52 If anyone has been disseized or dispossessed by us of lands, castles, liberties or of his rights, without lawful judgment of his peers, it shall immediately be restored to him. And if dispute should arise over this, then let it be settled by judgment of the twenty-five barons, as mentioned below in the security clause. For all those things of which anyone was disseized or dispossessed during the reign of King Henry our father or King Richard our brother, which we hold in our hand or which others hold, which we ought to warrant, we will have respite during the crusaders' term, excepting those cases when a plea was begun or an inquest made on our order before we took the cross; but when we have returned from our pilgrimage, or if by chance we do not go on our pilgrimage, we will immediately do full justice.

53 *Eundem autem respectum habebimus, et eodem modo, de justicia exhibenda de forestis deafforestandis vel remansuris forestis, quas Henricus pater noster vel Ricardus frater noster afforestaverunt, et de custodiis terrarum quae sunt de alieno feodo, cujusmodi custodias hucusque habuimus occasione feodi quod aliquis de nobis tenuit per servitium militare, et de abbatiis quae fundatae fuerint in feodo alterius quam nostro, in quibus dominus feodi dixerit se jus habere; et cum redierimus, vel si remanserimus a peregrinatione nostra, super hiis conquerentibus plenam justiciam statim exhibebimus.*

53 We shall have the same respite, and in the same manner, in doing justice on disafforesting or retaining those forests that Henry our father or Richard our brother afforested, and concerning wardships of lands which are part of another fee, wardships which we have held by reason of a fee which someone held of us by knight service, and of abbeys which were founded on a fee other than ours, in which the lord of the fee has claimed his right. And when we return, or if we do not go on our pilgrimage, we will immediately do full justice to those complaining about these things.

54   *Nullus capiatur nec imprisonetur propter appellum foeminae de morte alterius quam viri sui.*

54   No man shall be arrested or imprisoned because of the appeal of a woman for the death of anyone other than her husband.

55   *Omnes fines qui injuste et contra legem terrae facti sunt nobiscum, et omnia amerciamenta facta injuste et contra legem terrae, omnino condonentur, vel fiat inde per judicium viginti quinque baronum de quibus fit mentio inferius in securitate pacis, vel per judicium majoris partis eorumdem, una cum praedicto Stephano Cantuariensi archiepiscopo, si interesse poterit, et aliis quos secum ad hoc vocare voluerit. Et si interesse non poterit, nihilominus procedat negotium sine eo, ita quod, si aliquis vel aliqui de praedictis viginti quinque baronibus fuerint in simili querela, amoveantur quantum ad hoc judicium, et alii loco eorum per residuos de eisdem viginti quinque, tantum ad hoc faciendum electi et jurati substituantur.*

55   All fines which were made with us unjustly and contrary to the law of the land and all amercements made unjustly and contrary to the law of the land shall be completely remitted, or shall be settled by the twenty-five barons mentioned below in the security clause, or by the judgment of the majority of them, together with the aforementioned Stephen, Archbishop of Canterbury, if he can be present, and others such as he may wish to bring with him for this purpose. And if it is not possible for him to attend, let the business proceed without him, provided that if any one or more of the twenty-five barons are in such a suit, they shall be removed from this particular judgment, and shall be replaced in this case only by others chosen and sworn in by the twenty-five.

56   *Si nos dissaisivimus vel elongavimus Walenses de terris vel libertatibus vel rebus aliis, sine legali judicio parium suorum, in Anglia vel in Wallia, eis statim reddantur; et si contentio super hoc orta fuerit, tunc inde fiat in Marchia per judicium parium suorum, de tenementis Angliae secundum legem Angliae, de tenementis Walliae secundum legem Walliae, de tenementis Marchiae secundum legem Marchiae. Idem facient Walenses nobis et nostris.*

56   If we have disseized or deprived Welshmen of lands or liberties or other things without lawful judgment of their peers, in England or in Wales, they are to be returned to them immediately. And if a dispute arises about this, then it is to be settled in the March by judgment of their peers, for English tenements according to the law of England, for Welsh tenements according to the law of Wales, for tenements of the March according to the laws of the March. And the Welsh will do the same to us and ours.

57 *De omnibus autem illis de quibus aliquis Walensium dissaisitus fuerit vel elongatus sine legali judicio parium suorum, per Henricum regem patrem nostrum vel Ricardum regem fratrem nostrum, quae nos in manu nostra habemus, vel quae alii tenent quae nos oporteat warantizare, respectum habebimus usque ad communem terminum crucesignatorum, illis exceptis de quibus placitum motum fuit vel inquisitio facta per praeceptum nostrum ante susceptionem crucis nostrae: cum autem redierimus, vel si forte remanserimus a peregrinatione nostra, statim eis inde plenam justiciam exhibebimus, secundum leges Walensium et partes praedictas.*

57 However, with regard to all of the possessions of which any Welshman has been disseized or dispossessed without the lawful judgment of his peers, by King Henry our father, or King Richard our brother, and which we have in our hand, or which others hold which we ought to warrant, we will have respite for the common crusaders' term, except in cases where a plea was started or an inquest held by our instruction before we took the cross; however, when we return, or if by chance we do not go on crusade, then we will immediately do justice according to the laws of Wales and the parts previously mentioned.

58 *Nos reddemus filium Lewelini statim, et omnes obsides de Wallia, et cartas quae nobis liberatae fuerunt in securitatem pacis.*

58 We will immediately restore the son of Llywelyn and all the hostages from Wales, and charters that were delivered to us as security for peace.

59 *Nos faciemus Alexandro regi Scottorum de sororibus suis, et obsidibus reddendis, et libertatibus suis, et jure suo, secundum formam in qua faciemus aliis baronibus nostris Angliae, nisi aliter esse debeat per cartas quas habemus de Willelmo patre ipsius, quondam rege Scottorum; et hoc erit per judicium parium suorum in curia nostra.*

59 We will deal with Alexander, King of the Scots, regarding the return of his sisters and hostages and his liberties and rights in accordance with the way we deal with our other barons of England, unless it should be otherwise under the charters which we have from his father, William, former King of Scots. And this will be by judgment of his peers in our court.

60 *Omnes autem istas consuetudines praedictas et libertates quas nos concessimus in regno nostro tenendas quantum ad nos pertinet erga nostros, omnes de regno nostro, tam clerici quam laici, observent quantum ad se pertinent erga suos.*

60 All the previously mentioned customs and liberties which we have granted in our kingdom as far as we are concerned with regard to our own men, shall be observed by all men of our realm, both clergy and laity, as far as they are concerned with regard to their own men.

61 *Cum autem pro Deo, et ad emendationem regni nostri, et ad melius sopiendum discordiam inter nos et barones nostros ortam, haec omnia praedicta concesserimus, volentes ea integra et firma stabilitate in perpetuum gaudere, facimus et concedimus eis securitatem subscriptam; videlicet quod barones eligant viginti quinque barones de regno quos voluerint, qui debeant pro totis viribus suis observare, tenere, et facere observari, pacem et libertats quas ei concessimus, et hac praesenti carta nostra confirmavimus, ita scilicet quod, si nos, vel justiciarius noster, vel ballivi nostri, vel aliquis de ministris nostris, in aliquo erga aliquem deliquerimus, vel aliquem articulorum pacis aut securitatis transgressi fuerimus, et delictum ostensum fuerit quatuor baronibus de praedictis viginti quinque baronibus, illi quatuor barones accedant ad nos vel ad justiciarium nostrum, si fuerimus extra regnum, proponentes nobis excessum: petent ut excessum, illum sine dilatione faciamus emendari. Et si nos excessum non emendaverimus, vel, si fuerimus extra regnum, justiciarius noster non emendaverit infra tempus quadraginta dierum computandum a tempore quo monstratum fuerit nobis vel justiciario nostro si extra*

61 Since we have granted all these things for God and for the correction of our kingdom, and for the better settlement of the discord that has arisen between us and our barons, wishing these things to be enjoyed with full and firm stability in perpetuity, we make and grant them the following security: namely, that the barons are to choose twenty-five barons of the realm, whoever they wish, who with all their strength should observe, uphold and cause to be observed the peace and liberties which we have granted to them and confirmed to them in this present charter, so that if we or our justiciar, or our bailiffs, or any other of our officers shall in any way offend against anyone, or transgress against any of the articles of peace or security, and the offence has been shown to four of the said twenty-five barons, those four are to go to us, or our justiciar if we are out of the kingdom, setting forth the offence and demand that it be set right without delay. And if within the space of forty days of being shown the offence, we do not set right or if we are out of the realm, our justiciar does not set it right, the said four barons are to refer the case to the rest of the twenty-

regnum fuerimus, praedicti quatuor barones referant causam illam ad residuos de illis viginti quinque baronibus, et illi viginti quinque barones cum communia totius terrae distringent et gravabunt nos modis omnibus quibus poterunt, scilicet per captionem castrorum, terrarum, possessionum et aliis modis quibus poterunt, donec fuerit emendatum secundum arbitrium eorum, salva persona nostra et reginae nostrae et liberorum nostrorum; et cum fuerit emendatum intendent nobis sicut prius fecerunt. Et quicumque voluerit de terra juret quod ad praedicta omnia exsequenda parebit mandatis praedictorum viginti quinque baronum, et quod gravabit nos pro posse suo cum ipsis, et nos publice et libere damus licentiam jurandi cuilibet qui jurare voluerit, et nulli umquam jurare prohibebimus. Omnes autem illos de terra qui per se et sponte sua noluerint jurare viginti quinque baronibus de distringendo et gravando nos cum eis, faciemus jurare eosdem de mandato nostrosicut praedictum est. Et si aliquis de viginti quinque baronibus decesserit, vel a terra recesserit, vel aliquo alio modo impeditus fuerit, quo minus ista praedicta possent exsequi, qui residui fuerint de praedictis viginti quinque baronibus eligant alium loco ipsius, pro arbitrio suo, qui simili modo erit juratus quo et ceteri. In omnibus autem quae istis viginti quinque committuntur exsequenda, si forte ipsi viginti quinque praesentes fuerint, et inter se super re aliqua discordaverint, vel aliqui ex eis summoniti nolint vel nequeant interesse, ratum habeatur et firmum quod major pars eorum qui praesentes fuerint providerit,

five barons, and those twenty-five barons, with the community of the whole realm shall distrain and distress us in all ways possible, by taking castles, lands, possessions and in any other ways they can, until it has been put right in accordance with their judgment, saving our person and the persons of our queen and children. And once redress has been made let them obey us as they did before. And whoever of the land wishes may swear that he will obey the orders of the said twenty-five barons and with them distress us as much as he can, and we publicly and freely give permission to swear to whoever wishes to do so, and we will never prohibit anyone from swearing. Furthermore we will compel all those of the land who do not wish to swear with the twenty-five barons to distrain and distress us with them to swear as has been said. And if any of the twenty-five barons should die, or leave the land, or is in any other way prevented from doing his duties as previously mentioned, the remainder of the aforementioned twenty-five barons are to elect another in his place, by their own discretion, who will be sworn in the same manner as the rest. Furthermore, in everything that has been entrusted to the twenty-five barons to undertake, if it should happen that the twenty-five are present and disagree among themselves on anything, or if any of them, having been summoned, will not or cannot attend, whatever the majority of those present shall provide or command shall be considered as fixed and binding, as if all the twenty-five had agreed to it. And the aforementioned twenty-

vel praeceperit ac si omnes viginti quinque in hoc consensissent; et praedicti viginti quinque jurent quod omnia antedicta fideliter observabunt, et pro toto posse suo facient observari. Et nos nihil impetrabimus ab aliquo, per nos nec per alium, per quod aliqua istarum concessionum et libertatum revocetur vel minuatur; et, si aliquid tale impetratum fuerit, irritum sit et inane et numquam eo utemur per nos nec per alium.

five swear that they will faithfully observe all the aforesaid and cause it to be observed to their fullest ability. And we will ask nothing of anyone, either ourselves or through anyone else, through which any of these grants and liberties shall be revoked or diminished. And if any such thing shall be obtained, let it be null and void and we will never make use of it, through ourselves or through anyone else.

62   *Et omnes malas voluntates, indignationes, et rancores, ortos inter nos et homines nostros, clericos et laicos, a tempore discordiae, plene omnibus remisimus et condonavimus. Praeterea omnes trangressiones factas occasione ejusdem discordiae, a Pascha anno regni nostri sextodecimo usque ad pacem reformatam, plene remisimus omnibus, clericis et laicis, et quantum ad nos pertinet plene condonavimus. Et insuper fecimus eis litteras testimoniales patentes domini Stephani Cantuariensis archiepiscopi, domini Henrici Dublinensis archiepiscopi, et episcoporum praedictorum et magistri Pandulfi, super securitate ista et concessionibus praefatis.*

62   And we have fully remitted and pardoned all ill-will, indignation and rancour that has arisen between us and our men, clergy and laity, during the time of discord. Moreover, we have fully remitted to all men, clergy and laity, all the trangressions committed as the result of that discord between Easter in the sixteenth year of our reign until the establishment of peace, and as far as we are concerned, they are completely forgiven. And in addition we have had letters patent made by Lord Stephen, Archbishop of Canterbury, Lord Henry, Archbishop of Dublin, and the aforesaid bishops, and Master Pandulf testifying to this security and the aforesaid grants.

63 *Quare volumus et firmiter praecipimus quod Anglicana ecclesia libera sit et quod homines in regno nostro habeant et teneant omnes praefatas libertates, jura, et concessiones, bene et in pace, libere et quiete, plene et integre, sibi et haeredibus suis, de nobis et haeredibus nostris, in omnibus rebus et locis, in perpetuum, sicut praedictum est. Juratum est autem tam ex parte nostra quam ex parte baronum, quod haec omnia supradicta bona fide et sine malo ingenio observabuntur. Testibus supradictis et multis aliis. Data per manum nostram in prato quod vocatur Ronimed, inter Windlesoram et Stanes, quinto decimo die Junii, anno regni nostri decimo septimo.*

63 Wherefore we wish and firmly command that the English Church shall be free and that men in our kingdom have and hold all the aforesaid liberties, rights and grants, well and in peace, freely and quietly, fully and completely, for themselves and their heirs of us and our heirs, in all things and in all places, in perpetuity as has been said. This has been sworn to both on our behalf and on behalf of the barons, that all the previously mentioned things shall be observed in good faith and without evil intent. Witnessed by the above-mentioned and many others. Given by our hand in the meadow called Runnymede, between Windsor and Staines, on the fifteenth day of June, in the seventeenth year of our reign.

APPENDIX II
THE MEN OF MAGNA CARTA

When Magna Carta was issued in June 1215, twenty-seven men were named in the preamble as follows (and in this order), as having advised the king on its composition. These men were effectively the witnesses to the charter. Most of them had a history of loyal service to the king, which highlights the fact that the charter was granted explicitly to the king's faithful subjects, and its privileges were to be withheld from his enemies.

SMALL CAPITALS indicate cross-references.

Stephen, Archbishop of Canterbury,
Primate of All England and Cardinal of the Holy Roman Church
(?1160–1228)

A famous scholar and theologian, Stephen Langton laid the foundations for English canon-law procedure. He was appointed Archbishop of Canterbury by Pope Innocent III in 1207, but this caused a major rupture between the pope and King John, resulting in the pope excommunicating John and placing England under Interdict. Langton did not take office until 1213. Although he is often considered the author of Magna Carta, Langton's role was probably more as mediator between the king and the barons, although the prominence given to its Church-related matters is doubtless down to him. When Innocent ordered Magna Carta annulled in 1215 and excommunicated the barons who would not accede, Langton refused to publish the excommunications. He was then suspended and forced out of England until 1216, when both Innocent III and John died. He resumed his position as archbishop until his death in 1228.

Henry, Archbishop of Dublin (d.1228)

Henry of London was one of the most important and controversial arch-bishops of Dublin in the thirteenth century. A close ally of King John, he ensured the loyalty of the Irish barons to the Crown. He exerted very strong power in the administration of Ireland and often aroused complaints for obstructing secular justice. Eventually in 1224 King Henry III replaced him with William Marshal the Younger (*see* Appendix III). Henry of London died in 1228 and was buried in the Cathedral Church of Holy Trinity, Dublin.

William, Bishop of London (d.1224)

A Norman churchman admitted to the service of King Henry II before 1182, William de Sainte-Mère-Église became one of the Plantagenet regime's most trusted servants. He followed Richard I to England and obtained the diocese of London. He was appointed special counsellor under King John, but he was exiled between 1208 and 1213 for taking the side of the pope in the fight over the Archbishopric of Canterbury. After John's death, he was a counsellor to Henry III, before retiring in 1221. He died three years later at St Osyth, Essex.

Peter, Bishop of Winchester (d.1238)

Born in Touraine, northern France, Peter des Roches was a long-time asso-ciate and servant of the Plantagenet dynasty. He was one of only two bish-ops to remain loyal to King John during the dispute with Pope Innocent III and the period of the Interdict, and he served as guardian to the king's eldest son, Henry. He would retain a close relationship with Henry when he suc-ceeded as king, but he became embroiled in a long-running dispute with another royal servant, HUBERT DE BURGH. As justiciar, des Roches overrode numerous legal processes, which were viewed as breaches of Magna Carta and which caused a baronial revolt. In April 1234 Henry III ordered him to

leave court. He died four years later at Farnham, Surrey. His heart was buried at Waverley Abbey, the rest of his body in Winchester Cathedral.

Jocelin, Bishop of Bath and Glastonbury (d.1242)

A royal clerk and a canon, Jocelin of Wells was one of John's main advisers during the dispute with Pope Innocent III over the appointment of STEPHEN Langton to the Archbishopric of Canterbury. After John's excommunication he sided with Langton and the barons, but together with PETER des Roches he anointed King Henry III and helped him to restore the crown's possessions. He was the brother of HUGH, BISHOP OF LINCOLN.

Hugh, Bishop of Lincoln (d.1235)

The brother of JOCELIN, Hugh of Wells served as a royal administrator until 1209, when he was elected Bishop of Lincoln. The election aroused papal suspicions of undue royal influence and STEPHEN Langton was appointed to investigate, causing a delay in Hugh's consecration. After King John was excommunicated, Hugh went into exile in France, where he remained until 1213. He was later employed by King Henry III to negotiate with Louis VIII.

Walter, Bishop of Worcester (d.1255)

Walter de Gray was one of the closest supporters of King John, who appointed him chancellor at a very young age. He was instrumental in delaying the papal bill of excommunication. As thanks for his good work in this matter he was elected Archbishop of York in 1215. During the Barons' War of 1215–17 he raised mercenaries from abroad on the king's behalf, and he remained prominent well into the reign of Henry III, working energetically both as churchman and diplomat.

William, Bishop of Coventry (d.1223)

Raised in London, William de Cornhill made his way into royal administration via the service of Henry II and remained a faithful servant of John, serving variously as judge, chamberlain and tax collector. Tirelessly (but fruitlessly) he negotiated with both the Welsh rebels and the English barons before Runnymede. Following the king's death, de Cornhill was also present at the Gloucester coronation of Henry III. He was remembered after his death as *vir simplex et liberalis, fidelis regi et utilis regno*: 'a simple and generous man, faithful to the king and useful to the realm'.

Benedict, Bishop of Rochester (d.1226)

Benedict of Sawston was Preceptor of St Paul's. It is possible that he studied in Paris under STEPHEN Langton, who recommended him for the election as Bishop of Rochester in December 1214. He was of greater service to the Crown after, rather than before, John's death, serving as a judge in South-East England before being sent to France in 1225 as an ambassador to negotiate the peace settlement with Louis VIII.

Master Pandulf, subdeacon and confidant of the lord pope (d.1226)

Pandulf Verraccio, Bishop of Norwich, was born in Rome and went to England as a papal legate on the orders of Innocent III, to receive John's submission following the Interdict. Pandulf subsequently remained close to the king, advising him during the conflict with the barons, among whom he was extremely unpopular thanks to his foreign background and offensively lavish habits. Highly active in the minority of Henry III, Pandulf was a crucial figure in the restoration of order following the Barons' War of 1215–17. He left England in 1221 and died in Rome five years later.

Brother Aymeric, Master of the Knights Templar in England (d.?1219)

Aymeric de St Maur was Master of the Order of the Knights Templar in England. The Templars were a wealthy, powerful and highly protected order of crusading monks, who owned prominent property in London. Aymeric was a steady financial supporter of John, and the king actually stayed in the Temple for a time in 1215. Over the period 1203 to 1206 the Templars had lent the king money for the ransom of soldiers captured in France and for mercenaries. In return, the king made several gifts to the Order, including the Isle of Lundy. Aymeric probably died in 1219, when he was succeeded by Alan Marcel.

William Marshal, Earl of Pembroke (*c.*1146–1219)

One of the most famous knights not only of his day but of all time, William Marshal's life was spent in the service of the Plantagenet family. Although he fell out with John during the king's pursuit of the de Briouze family, Marshal (sometimes called 'William the Marshal') returned to the fold and remained a loyal supporter of the Crown, taking charge of the person of Henry III after John's death and leading the war against Prince Louis of France, despite being around sixty years old at the time. A dramatic and highly self-serving 19,000-word Life of Marshal is, despite its obvious exaggerations and distortions, still one of the most enjoyable and interesting sources for this period of English history.

William, Earl of Salisbury (?1167–1226)

The bastard son of Henry II, William Longspée was recognized as a man with almost princely status. A brave and talented warrior, he fought with his half-brother Richard I in Normandy and served his other half-brother King John as a diplomat, also taking part in the burning of the French fleet in the River Zwin in 1213. Longspée commanded a division on the losing side at the

The effigy of William Marshal (*c.*1146–1219) atop his tomb, in London's Temple Church. Known as 'the greatest knight that ever lived', William, Earl of Pembroke, was loyal to all the Plantagenet kings he served. He advised John during the Magna Carta negotiations and played a crucial role in saving the reign of John's young son Henry III.

Battle of Bouvines the following year, despite having counselled John not to fight. He was captured and ransomed. Present at the king's side at Runnymede, he temporarily defected to the baronial cause when Louis invaded. This was a brief phase; Longspée soon returned to the king's ranks and was heavily involved in both the civil war and the peace negotiations for the Treaty of Lambeth in 1217. He continued to play a prominent military role in the minority government of Henry III, until his death in 1226.

William, Earl Warenne (d.1240)

Born in Normandy, William de Warenne, Earl of Surrey (usually referred to as Earl Warenne), was the son of Henry II's illegitimate brother Hamelin. He attempted to remain in favour with both Philip Augustus of France and John following the loss of Normandy, but he eventually threw in his lot with the English king. An active supporter of the Crown throughout John's reign, he was closely involved in the civil war and the negotiations with the barons before Runnymede. After John's death he briefly supported Prince Louis in the hope of regaining French lands lost in 1204, but he returned swiftly to the royal fold and played a prominent role in the reign of Henry III. Warenne was one of the few barons who witnessed Magna Carta both in 1215 and in 1237, at its reissue.

William, Earl of Arundel (*c.*1174–1221)

William d'Aubigny was a long-time associate of King John's, having fought with him in Normandy during Richard I's reign. He was involved in negotiations with STEPHEN Langton in 1209 and witnessed John's submission to the pope in 1213. Despite supporting John at Runnymede, in 1216 d'Aubigny went over to Louis's side, before turning his coat again following the Battle of Lincoln. He participated in the Fifth Crusade and died on his way home, near Rome.

Alan of Galloway, Constable of Scotland (before 1199–?1234)

A ferocious warrior, Alan had semi-princely powers in Galloway and territorial interests stretching from Northern England to the Kingdom of Norway. He assisted John in the subjugation of Ireland, but sided with Alexander II, King of Scots, during the war that followed the repudiation of Magna Carta.

Warin FitzGerald (d.1235)

Warin FitzGerald came from a family of hereditary chamberlains and served King John in the same capacity. His daughter Margaret, widow of the Earl of Devon, was forcefully married by King John to the military captain Falkes de Breauté. Margaret later pleaded to annul the marriage, appealing to Clause 8 of Magna Carta, which forbade the forced marriage of a widow. Divorce was not granted, but she remained in Henry III's custody.

Peter FitzHerbert (d.1235)

John nominated Peter FitzHerbert as Baron of Barnstable, Devonshire. His other offices included serving as Governor of Pickering Castle and Sheriff of Yorkshire. Despite advising John at Runnymede, he later sided with the barons and his lands were confiscated, only to be returned to him on the accession of Henry III. He died in 1235 and was buried at Reading.

Hubert de Burgh, Seneschal of Poitou (c.1170–1243)

Born into a family of minor landowners, de Burgh's spectacular rise was reward for his vigorous and loyal service to John and Henry III. Legend – and Shakespeare – has him refusing to castrate Arthur of Brittany (John's nephew and rival), contrary to John's orders, in 1203. Captured and ransomed at Chinon in 1205, he subsequently returned to England and built up

a substantial landholding in the South and East of the country. He was appointed Seneschal of Poitou during the failed Bouvines campaign and played a prominent role at the king's side during the negotiations for Magna Carta. Hubert de Burgh held Dover Castle successfully against Prince Louis in 1216–17, led the fleet at the Battle of Sandwich, and subsequently played a prominent, if disruptive, role as justiciar and rival to PETER des Roches during the early reign of Henry III.

Hugh de Neville (d.1234)

Son of a family of unpopular royal foresters, de Neville was raised at court with Richard I and knew him and John well. He went on crusade with Richard and was present at the siege of Jaffa. He became one of John's closest advisers, but before the king's death de Neville joined the baronial party, which temporarily cost him his office and lands. Under Henry III he reconciled with the Crown and was reappointed chief justice of the forests.

Matthew FitzHerbert (*c.*1166–*c.*1231)

Matthew FitzHerbert was from Gloucestershire. His name appears repeatedly as High Sheriff of Sussex: from 1211 to 1215, in 1218, and from 1219 to 1224.

Thomas Basset (d.1220)

An associate of John from his days as Count of Mortain, Basset was one of the men excommunicated for his treacherous behaviour during Richard I's absence on crusade. During the Barons' War he remained loyal to John, who compensated him with Warwick Castle and the estates of several rebel knights. He was the brother of ALAN BASSET.

THE MEN OF MAGNA CARTA

Hubtus de burgo dis-
calciatus ꞇ camisia
solū an̄ altare de ꝗto-
na mortē orando gᵃ-
ta. Aduenuit enī cui̅es
lond hostes eius

Hoc ꞇ greͭ oꝛ duobꝫ alui̅ꝰ
locis seqntibꝫ .s. apꝺ boseu q̄
bustu. ꞇ capella apꝺ deuisas.

Alan Basset (d.1232)

A noted diplomat under Richard I, Basset continued his loyalty into John's reign, frequently witnessing royal charters in England and France and receiving rewards for good service, including immunity from paying scutage (the feudal payment in lieu of actual military service). Basset fought on the winning side at the Battle of Lincoln (1217), and joined the government of Henry III thereafter, travelling to France to negotiate terms for peace in 1220. He remained in royal service until his death. He was the brother of THOMAS BASSET.

Philip d'Aubigny (d.?1236)

A baron with interests on both sides of the Channel before 1204, d'Aubigny took the part of John following the loss of Normandy and fought at Poitou in the Bouvines campaign. During the Barons' War he was awarded the title 'Commander of the Knights of Christ'. D'Aubigny fought at both the Battle of Lincoln (1217) and the naval Battle of Sandwich (1217), and he subsequently took responsibility for the military education of Henry III. He died in Jerusalem after joining the Fifth Crusade.

Robert de Roppel (dates unknown)

An obscure character, also known variously as Robert de Roppeley, de Ros and de Rokkeley, he seems to have served the Crown as Sheriff of Norfolk. After the signing of Magna Carta he joined the barons and was taken prisoner by King John's forces at Rochester Castle in 1216.

John Marshal (d.?1235)

A nephew of WILLIAM MARSHAL, Earl of Pembroke, Sir John fought with his uncle in Normandy and subsequently served King John in a variety of

capacities in Ireland. After Runnymede, Marshal was sent to Rome as an ambassador, but returned in time to take part in the battles of Lincoln and Sandwich in 1217. He retained his Irish interests during Henry III's reign, remaining largely loyal to the Crown until he died.

John FitzHugh (dates unknown)

John FitzHugh belonged to a Yorkshire family known as the FitzHughs of Ravensworth. He served as a judge and was a firm adherent of King John.

APPENDIX III
THE ENFORCERS OF MAGNA CARTA

M atthew Paris (*c.*1200–59), in his *Chronica Majora*, lists the twenty-five barons (in this order) who were appointed to enforce Magna Carta 1215.[1] Under the terms of Clause 61, these men were empowered to 'distrain and distress [the king] in all ways possible' if he or his officials broke the terms of the charter and did not provide remedy within forty days. Another copy of this list, now held in Lambeth Palace, included the number of knights that each of the twenty-five barons (with the exception of the Mayor of London) was expected to bring to war in the event of the security clause being activated.[2]

SMALL CAPITALS indicate cross-references.

Richard, Earl of Clare (d.1217)

Otherwise known as Richard de Clare, Earl of Hertford, a title he held from 1173, Richard was present at the coronations of both Richard I and John, although he enjoyed a closer relationship with the older brother than the younger. His power base was at Tonbridge Castle in Kent, and Richard was among the rebellious East Anglian barons; he may have been involved in the plot to kill John in 1212. His lands were seized during the Barons' War of 1215–17, and he was excommunicated by the pope. Richard died in November 1217, leaving as his heir a son, GILBERT, who was also named among the twenty-five.

William de Forz, Count of Aumale (?1190s–1241)

Aumale was a small town in Normandy, so in theory William's English title should have become obsolete when Philip Augustus reconquered the duchy. But it was obstinately maintained under King John and linked with the Lordship of Holderness in Yorkshire. William's mother, Hawisa, suffered the

blunt force of John's feudal extortion: when her husband (William's stepfather) died in 1212, she had to pay 5,000 marks to avoid being forced to remarry. Although raised mostly outside England, William came to the realm to claim his inheritance on Hawisa's death in 1214 and immediately found reason to join the baronial opposition. However, he switched to John's side in late summer 1215 and profited mightily from grants of confiscated rebel lands. William was a witness to the reissues of Magna Carta under Henry III in 1216 and 1225, but also caused significant political trouble during Henry's minority. He lived a relatively long and very active life before dying on his way to Jerusalem, on pilgrimage.

Geoffrey de Mandeville, Earl of Essex, Earl of Gloucester (d.1216)

De Mandeville was a wealthy baron whose responsibilities included being custodian of the Tower of London. He was driven to rebellion in 1214, when, after marrying the king's divorced first wife Isabel, Countess of Gloucester, he was browbeaten into agreeing to pay the monstrous sum of 20,000 marks for the privilege – by some distance the most outlandish of all John's feudal extortions. The debt was simply unpayable, and it was probably set at an impossible level so that John could seize back Gloucester lands that he had forfeited by separating from Isabel. De Mandeville was expected to bring 200 knights to oppose the king if the 'council of twenty-five' went to war to enforce Magna Carta – the only other baron contracted for so many was WILLIAM MARSHAL THE YOUNGER. De Mandeville's was a brief rebellion: he was killed at a tournament in London, in February 1216.

Saer de Quincy, Earl of Winchester (d.1219)

A major landowner on the Scottish borders, de Quincy was also an experienced soldier who fought with Richard the Lionheart and John in Normandy,

and who was captured by the French at Vaudreuil in 1203. Later he served John in Scotland, Ireland and Germany, worked as a royal justice, and was heavily involved in the work of the Exchequer. De Quincy witnessed both John's legal deposition against William de Briouze in 1210 and the king's submission to the pope in 1213. He took the cross with the king in March 1215, but turned on him weeks later, travelling to Scotland to stir up Alexander II for an invasion of England's North. A great friend and brother-in-arms of ROBERT FITZWALTER, de Quincy allowed the rebels to use his lands at Brackley to renounce their homage before the march on London in May 1215. Later, he was among the party of barons who invited Prince Louis to invade England. Captured at the Battle of Lincoln (1217), de Quincy returned to loyalty and was present during the council that granted Magna Carta 1217; but he left the realm on crusade eighteen months later and died in Damietta, to be buried in Acre.

Henry de Bohun, Earl of Hereford (*c.*1175–1220)
Hereditary Constable of England, de Bohun was the nephew of William I (the Lion), King of Scots, to whom he was sent on diplomatic business shortly after John's coronation. Disputes with John, stemming in part from an argument with the king's half-brother William Longspée (*see* Appendix II) over Trowbridge Castle in Wiltshire, caused de Bohun to side with the rebels, and all his lands were confiscated by the king. He went back to John's side late in 1215, then switched once again to support Prince Louis against Henry III. Captured at the Battle of Lincoln in 1217, he made peace with the new regime and died on pilgrimage to the Holy Land in 1220.

Roger Bigod, Earl of Norfolk (*c.*1143–1221)
The Bigod family had a history of conflict with Plantagenet kings dating back to Roger's father, Hugh Bigod, and his involvement in the 'Great War'

against Henry II of 1173–4. Despite this, Roger was close to Richard I and very active in the service of King John, taking part in campaigns in Poitou, Scotland, Ireland and Wales. It may have been John's grinding financial demands that lay behind Roger's decision to join the rebels, as part of the bloc of East Anglian barons. Whatever his reasons, Bigod remained unreconciled with John at the king's death and only returned to loyalty in 1217, once it was clear that William Marshal, Earl of Pembroke (*see* Appendix II), and the supporters of Henry III had won the war. His heir was HUGH BIGOD. The Bigod earls remained vastly powerful for several generations before dying out in the early fourteenth century.

Robert de Vere, Earl of Oxford (d.1221)

Another eastern rebel, de Vere was named by Roger of Wendover as one of the prime movers of dissent against John's regime. His actions seem to have been inspired more by pragmatism than deep rebellious commitment – he was one of the barons who wavered back and forth between John and Prince Louis in 1216 and was active as a royal judge following the victory of the Plantagenet loyalists.

William Marshal the Younger (*c.*1190–1231)

William experienced the rough end of John's kingship as a young man, when he was kept as a hostage at court for seven years, to guarantee the good behaviour of his father, the illustrious William Marshal, Earl of Pembroke (*see* Appendix II). Unlike the elder Marshal, the young man sided with the opposition in 1215–16 and was appointed the marshal of Prince Louis's army. But he switched sides early in the war and fought under his father at the Battle of Lincoln (1217). After his father's death early in Henry III's reign, Marshal set about expanding his family's possessions in Wales, Ireland and Southern England. He died suddenly and without offspring in 1231, leaving

his brothers – Richard, Gilbert, Walter and Anselm – as his successive heirs. None produced legitimate children, and in 1245 the Marshal estates were broken up among their sisters and heiresses.

Robert FitzWalter (d.1235)

FitzWalter was one of the rebel ringleaders from 1212, when he plotted with EUSTACE DE VESCI to have John murdered. A rich and powerful East Anglian, he had particularly close links to SAER DE QUINCY, whom he considered a brother and whose arms he bore on his seal. Argumentative and easily stirred to violence, FitzWalter led the widespread baronial refusal to fight alongside John during the Poitou and Bouvines campaigns of 1213–14. In May 1215 he declared himself Marshal of the Army of God and led the march on London. Despite his riches and his large following, FitzWalter failed to relieve the siege of Rochester Castle during the fighting in autumn 1215 and was captured during the Battle of Lincoln in 1217. After the war, he travelled with Saer de Quincy to Damietta on the Fifth Crusade. Unlike his friend, he survived, returning to England a much-changed man: he served Henry III's regime loyally until his death.

Gilbert de Clare (c.1180–1230)

The son and heir of RICHARD, EARL OF CLARE, Gilbert was around thirty-five years old in 1215 and had been guided by his rebellious father in his political activity during the preceding years. He sided with Prince Louis during the war following John's death, but switched sides to ally with William Marshal, Earl of Pembroke (see Appendix II), following the Battle of Lincoln (1217). Gilbert inherited the great Earldom of Gloucester from his mother Amicia but was never a very active political figure. Present at the reissue of Magna Carta by Henry III in 1225, he died in Brittany on campaign with the king five years later.

Eustace de Vesci (1169/70–1216)

De Vesci was a Northerner of considerable status, thanks to his marriage to an illegitimate daughter of William I (the Lion), King of Scots. One of the ringleaders of baronial rebellion from the very start, he was implicated deeply in the plot to assassinate John in 1212. Chroniclers, from William of Newburgh onwards, suggested that the root of such long-standing opposition was the king's lecherous designs on de Vesci's wife. Whether this was true or not, de Vesci was committed to rebellion early. He supported Prince Louis's invasion and was killed during the siege of Barnard Castle in County Durham, when an arrow was shot through his brain.

Hugh Bigod (d.1225)

The son and heir of ROGER BIGOD, Earl of Norfolk, Hugh inherited the earldom when his father died in 1221. He married Matilda, a daughter of William Marshal, Earl of Pembroke (*see* Appendix II). Bigod survived long enough to witness the reissue of Magna Carta in 1225 but died shortly afterwards.

William de Mowbray (*c.*1173–*c.*1224)

Although physically tiny, apparently no larger than a dwarf, de Mowbray was respected for his courage and generosity. He was an active warrior in the service of the king until 1215, when he joined with his fellow Northerners in rebellion. He remained in opposition until the Battle of Lincoln (1217), where he was captured, but he later made peace with the new regime.

The 'Mayor of London': Serlo the Mercer (dates unknown)

At the time of Magna Carta, the mayoralty was held by the textile dealer and property owner Serlo the Mercer, who kept houses across the city, including in the parish of St-Mary-le-Bow. Serlo served as mayor in 1215 and again

from 1216 to 1221. His support for the baronial opposition was crucial, since holding London was vital leverage in obtaining the charter of liberties from John. The only member of the twenty-five not expected to raise knights, Serlo was instead required to give the City of London over to baronial control if John contravened Magna Carta.[3]

William de Lanvallei (d.1217)

De Lanvallei was connected to ROBERT FITZWALTER by virtue of having married his niece. He was also Governor of Colchester Castle, over which he tussled with the Crown between 1214 and 1217, when he died while still in rebellion.

Robert de Ros (*c.*1182–1226/7)

A staunch Northerner, with estates in Yorkshire and Northumberland, de Ros was a regular companion of the king in the early years of John's reign, when he was even to be found at the royal gambling table. He witnessed John's submission to the pope and was still enjoying royal favour and holding royal office in April 1215. Somehow dragged into opposition very late in the day, de Ros remained estranged until the autumn of 1217. He witnessed the 1225 reissue of Magna Carta and then retired to live out the last months of his life as a monk.

John de Lacy, Constable of Chester (*c.*1192–1240)

A young man at the time of Magna Carta, de Lacy only inherited his father's massive estates in Northern England in return for a enormous levy of 7,000 marks. He took the cross with John on 4 March 1215, for which he was granted a substantial reduction in his debts to the Crown. Rebelling only in the final three weeks before Magna Carta was granted, de Lacy never seemed

greatly convinced by the cause, flitting back and forth between king and rebels. After reconciliation with Henry III's regime in 1217, he went to Damietta on crusade, before returning to play a full part in the new reign. He was one of the few men of 1215 (RICHARD DE MONTFICHET was another) who also went on to witness both the 1225 and 1237 reissues of Magna Carta.

Richard de Percy (d.1244)

A young Northerner who refused to serve on John's Bouvines campaign in 1214, de Percy entered active opposition during the summer of 1215. He brought Yorkshire under the obedience of Prince Louis in 1216 and was only reconciled to the Crown relatively late, in November 1217. Apparently one of the less wealthy barons, he was only expected to bring ten knights in the event that the council of twenty-five declared war on John. Towards the end of his life, de Percy was witness to the 1237 reconfirmation of Magna Carta.

John FitzRobert (d.1244)

Both a Northern baron and a man of substance in East Anglia, FitzRobert's landholdings reached from Warkworth and Rothbury in Northumberland to Clavering in Essex. His cousin was a fellow member of the twenty-five, JOHN DE LACY. Given that he had served as a royal sheriff, FitzRobert is a good example of a rebel knitted into the ranks of the opposition by a number of parallel links of territory and family connection.

William Malet (c.1175–1215)

A crusading companion of Richard the Lionheart, Malet was a significant landholder in Somerset, far from the main geographical centres of rebellion in the North and East of England. He found himself in serious debt to the Crown in the years before Magna Carta, owing 2,000 marks in 1214, which

Apres son regná Henry le terz sun fiz. lvi. aunz. si
fust de .ix. aunz de age quant fust coroné. e en son
tens fust la batáylle de Euesham. ou fust occys syr
Symund de munfort. e sun fiz henry. e syre hugh le des
penser e muz des barons e des cheualers de Engle
tere. puis mourst cyl henry le roy. e gist a Westmuster.

he attempted to have cancelled in return for military service in France. This tension probably explains his decision to join the rebels in the summer of 1215, although the fact that he had previously served as a sheriff and had not shirked his military duties suggests that he may have been one of the more moderate barons among the twenty-five.

Geoffrey de Say (c.1155–1230)

Geoffrey de Say took part in military campaigns for the king in Ireland. He subsequently inherited his father's lands across South-East England and the Home Counties, for which he paid only a moderate fine. However, he joined the baronial opposition nonetheless and was briefly deprived of his lands in October 1215. De Say made peace with Henry III's regime in 1217 and subsequently went twice on pilgrimage, to the Holy Land and then to Santiago de Compostela in Spain.

Roger de Montbegon (d.1226)

A landowner in Lincolnshire and Lancashire, and at one point the keeper of Nottingham Castle, de Montbegon refused to pay scutage to the king or do military service in the years leading up to Magna Carta. Erroneously named Roger de Mowbray by Matthew Paris and in the Lambeth Palace Library manuscript, de Montbegon was expected to bring just ten knights to any punitive military action taken by the twenty-five in the case of John breaking the terms of the charter.

William de Huntingfield (d.?1225)

With lands scattered from Essex and Suffolk to Lincolnshire and Lancaster, de Huntingfield was an active supporter of King John until the defeat at Bouvines in 1214: he served as a justice in Eyre in 1208–9 and as Sheriff of

Norfolk and Suffolk the following year. In spring 1215, however, he went into opposition and was active in East Anglia during the Barons' War of 1215–17, taking control of the region on behalf of Prince Louis. Seemingly a bird-lover, he appears in the records early in John's reign seeking favour from the king with gifts of a falcon and six 'beautiful Norwegian hawks'.

Richard de Montfichet (c.1190–1267)

One of the few men to live through both the Barons' Wars of the thirteenth century (1215–17 and 1264–7), de Montfichet came of age just in time to travel with King John to Poitou in 1214. His family were hereditary custodians of royal forest land in Essex, which de Montfichet secured during Magna Carta negotiations, but which was withdrawn during the subsequent fighting, only to be restored to him in 1217 by the young Henry III's government. Like JOHN DE LACY, he witnessed both the 1225 and 1237 reissues of Magna Carta. Perhaps having learned his lesson during the troubles of his early days, he remained neutral during the wars between Henry III and Simon de Montfort, Earl of Leicester, in the 1260s.

William d'Aubigny (d.1236)

William d'Aubigny was Lord of Belvoir in Leicestershire, and he served as a sheriff in three different counties. Despite being critical of the Crown, he remained neutral for a long time during the rebellion against John, eventually joining the rebels in time to be among the twenty-five barons. He subsequently led the defence of Rochester Castle during its siege (October–November 1215), where he was said to have dissuaded a crossbowman from assassinating John from the castle's battlements. D'Aubigny was imprisoned in Corfe Castle following the fall of Rochester Castle, but he was released on John's death. He joined Henry III's side and was a commander at the Battle of Lincoln in 1217.

prorupit de castro cum suis audacter in medium hostium. sed
ab irruentibus in eum legionibus captus est, et adductus domini per
probitatem balistariorum ac militum suorum liberatus est, et ad suos
reductus. Interea moles totius exercitus regis januis civitatis licet cum difficultate confractis villam ingrediens
audacter prorupit in hostes. Videres ibi ex ictibus gladiorum
igneas prosilire scintillas, et ad modum tonitrui vel terre-
motus totam terram reboare ex congressibus confligentium.
Sed tandem per regales quorum probitate equi in quibus sedebant
barones celeriter confossi sunt et ad instar porcorum jugu-
lati, pars baronum fuit penitus infirmata. Saepe enim equi
corruerunt in terram interfecti, sessores eorum capiebantur
cum non esset qui eos liberaret. Tandem cum regis milicia baronibus penitus enervatis cepisset ex eis militum multitu-
dinem numerosam ac vinctis omnibus mancipasset, irruit
densis agminibus in comitem Perticensem circumvallando
eum undique et versum est in eum pondus belli. Sed demum cum im-
petum irruentium sustinere non potuit, hortati sunt ut se
redderet, ut vivus evadere posset. At ille cum juramento
horribiliter affirmavit quod se Anglicis aliquatenus nequaquam redderet, qui proprii regis proditores fuerunt. Et hiis au-
ditis irruit quidam de regalibus et per ocularium galee
caput ejus perforando cerebrum effudit, et mucro ejus per cerebrum sepe peragravit. Et corruens in terram nec dominum invo-
cavit nec verbum unum edidit. Sed in summo rancore et ira
ad inferos peregrinavit. Videntes igitur Galligene quod
maior eorum pars cecidisset, inierunt fugam tam pedites quam
equites sibi nimis dampnosam. Nam flagellum porte
australis per quam fugerunt quod ex transverso fuerat fab-
ricatum fugientes non mediocriter impedivit. Veniens quicumque
eorum aliquis adveniens et festinus nimis exire voluis-
set, oportebat eum ab equo descendere et portam aperire.
quo exeunte porta statim recludebatur flagello ut prius

tantum ex omnibus in tanti discrimine belli occisi referuntur.
His ita gestis invenerunt. De spoliis civitatis et ecclesiarum.
regii bellatores in plateis civitatis bigas plurimas
baronum et Francorum cum summariis et sarcinis, vasis argen-
teis, et varia supellectili simul cum utensilibus onustas
que omnia in usus eorum sine contradictione cesserunt. Spolia-
ta itaque civitate universa usque ad ultimum quadrantem ec-
clesias omnis totius urbis consequenter spoliantes, archas etiam cum
almariolis securibus et malleis confregerunt, rapientes
in eis aurum et argentum, pannos diversi coloris ac mu-
liebria ornamenta, anulos aureos, cum ciphis et lapidi-
bus preciosis. Nec etiam ecclesia cathedralis hanc pestem evasit
quin subiret iudicium aliarum. Datum enim erat militibus
in mandatis a legato, ut etiam canonicos omnes tractarent
ut excommunicatos, et sicut tales qui hostes fuerunt
Romane ecclesie ac regis Anglie ab inicio guerre
mote. Fuit autem ulterius per causa sufficiente aliquid habere quod
auferri posset sicut consuetudo est Romanis de levi causas
adinvenire, ubi materia pecunie subiacet malignantibus.
Precentor autem ecclesie illius Galfridus scilicet de Drepinges, xi.
milia marcas argenti se insolabiliter doluit amisis-
se. Tandem cum etiam mercimoniorum genera rapuissent ita quod
nichil in aliquo domus angulo remansit intactum, reversi sunt singuli ad dominos suos divites effecti. Atque ab omnibus
pace regis Henrici per civitatem denunciata, epulabantur
et bibebant cum iocunditate. Facta est autem ista
belli congressio quam in opprobrium Lodowici ac baronum
nundinas appellant, xiiii. kl. iunii, sabbato scilicet in ebdomada
pentecostes hora inter primam et terciam me-
dia. Sed ante horam nonam a bonis negociatoribus sunt
omnia consummata. Verum ex matronis civitatis aliquae
fuerunt aquis submerse. Que ut scandalum et ludibri-
um evitarent, pueros et supellectiles ingresse naviculas cum

APPENDIX IV

TIMELINE
800 YEARS OF MAGNA CARTA

1100

King Henry I, on becoming King of England, grants a charter of liberties promising, among other matters, freedom for the Church and to keep peace in the land.

1154

Henry II accedes to the English throne and grants a charter of liberties to mark his coronation.

1166

The Assize of Clarendon extends royal law deep into local areas, with crimes investigated via the General Eyre.

1170

Archbishop Thomas Becket is murdered in Canterbury Cathedral, the culmination of a dispute with Henry II over royal attempts to bring secular law to bear on churchmen.

1173–4

The 'Great War', a baronial rebellion, ends in Henry II's favour. There is a massive programme of castle demolition and seizure, and the Treaty of Falaise subjects Scots to English overlordship.

1189

Henry II dies, to be succeeded by his son Richard I 'the Lionheart'. By the end of the year Richard departs on crusade, paid for by heavy taxation and the sale of public offices.

1192

Richard I is captured while returning from the Holy Land and imprisoned by the Holy Roman Emperor Henry VI until 1194, only to be released on payment of a massive 150,000-mark ransom.

1199

11 April. Richard I dies while commanding the siege of the castle at Châlus-Chabrol.

27 May: Richard's brother John, who had fomented rebellion in the Plantagenet Empire during Richard's absence and imprisonment, is crowned King of England.

1200

John agrees unfavourable terms with Philip II (Augustus) of France in the Treaty of Le Goulet, earning himself the demeaning nickname of 'Softsword'.

1202

John loses Anjou, Maine, Touraine and other Plantagenet lands on the continent to Philip Augustus and his allies.

1203

c. April: Arthur of Brittany, John's nephew and a rival for the throne backed by Philip Augustus of France, disappears while in John's captivity, probably murdered.

December: John leaves Normandy for England, while the duchy is threatened by Philip Augustus.

1204

Normandy falls to Philip Augustus, a severe blow to John.

The French invasion of Gascony reduces the Plantagenet 'Empire' to a small strip of Aquitaine.

1205

13 July: Hubert Walter, Archbishop of Canterbury, dies; John refuses to accept Pope Innocent III's election of Stephen Langton as his replacement.

John launches an abortive invasion of Poitou, which ends in stalemate and a two-year truce with France.

1207

John intensifies the financial expropriations from his barons, through taxation, feudal dues and the proceeds of legal processes.

1208

March: England is placed under Interdict by Pope Innocent III in the escalating dispute with John over Langton's appointment: churches fall silent, and John takes the opportunity to seize Church wealth. John also begins pursuit of William de Briouze for non-payment of debt.

John pays homage to Philip II of France, in a scene from the richly illustrated *Chroniques de France ou de St Denis*, created some time between 1330 and 1350. John had paid homage to Philip as part of his plotting to wrest Plantagenet land from King Richard; but thereafter John's failure to conserve the Plantagenet Empire against Philip's ambitions cemented the weak reputation of a king known as 'Softsword'.

N celle annee le iour de
uant la premiere kl. de iu
gnet uint en france li rois
iehans dengleterre. Li rois
plebures le rut moult hement et a

1209

August: William I (the Lion), King of Scots, submits to John at the Treaty of Norham; the hostages include his two daughters.

November: In the continuing royal–papal stand-off, John is excommunicated by Pope Innocent III.

1210

John leads a military campaign in Ireland, in pursuit of William de Briouze.

De Briouze's wife, Matilda, and son are starved to death in prison, after attempting to negotiate with John on his behalf.

1211

March–July: John invades Wales and forces Llywelyn ap Iorwerth of Gwynedd to recognize him as overlord.

September: William de Briouze dies in exile in France.

1212

August: A plot to murder John is led by two disgruntled barons, Eustace de Vesci and Robert FitzWalter, who flee abroad and are declared outlaws. John aborts attempts to muster an army to regain his continental empire.

1213

April: Philip Augustus of France and his son, Prince Louis, plan an invasion of England to topple the excommunicated John.

15 May: In the face of the French threat, John publicly backs down in the dispute with Innocent III, submitting and accepting papal overlordship in return for the lifting of the Interdict.

30 May: English ships burn the French fleet in the River Zwin, and the invasion of England is abandoned.

2 November: John meets the still intractable Northern barons in an attempt to gain support for continental war.

1214

January: John demands from Geoffrey de Mandeville, Earl of Essex, an astonishing 20,000 marks for the right to marry the king's former wife, Isabel of Gloucester.

February: John sails for La Rochelle to join a two-pronged attack on Philip Augustus.

27 July: The coalition of John's allies is soundly beaten by Philip Augustus at the Battle of Bouvines.

13 October: The defeated John leaves France for England, where baronial unrest, especially in the North, is reaching breaking point.

Between October and late spring 1215, the so-called Unknown Charter, demanding reforms, is compiled.

1215

January: A conference between John and the barons in London breaks up with the latter demanding reconfirmation of Henry I's coronation charter.

4 March: John takes the cross, hoping that crusader status with the pope will strengthen his hand domestically and internationally.

25 April: John fails to meet barons at Northampton to respond to their demands (perhaps those contained in the Unknown Charter).

5 May: Baronial opponents formally renounce their feudal loyalty to King John at Brackley, Northamptonshire.

12 May: John orders the besieging of rebel castles.

17 May: London is captured by rebels under Robert FitzWalter, who styles himself 'Marshal of the Army of God'.

10 June: Negotiations between royal and rebel parties begin at Runnymede. John accepts a draft document, the 'Articles of the Barons', as terms for negotiation of a peace.

15 June: John grants Magna Carta at Runnymede. It contains a range of royal promises, breach of which is liable to enforcement (by military means) by a named group of twenty-five barons.

19 June: Formerly rebellious barons signal their acceptance of Magna Carta by renewing their homage to the king.

Mid-July: John writes to Pope Innocent III requesting annulment of Magna Carta. On 24 August, the pope declares the charter null and void and excommunicates rebel barons and the citizens of London.

September: War with the barons resumes. John lays siege to Rochester Castle, held by Archbishop Langton. Barons ask Prince Louis to invade.

October: Northern barons pay homage to Alexander II, King of Scots, who is invited to invade England.

30 November: Rochester Castle falls to John.

December: The first French troops begin to arrive in England.

1216

January–March: John's determined offensive in the North and East Anglia begins successfully; but his ships fail to blockade the French invasion fleet across the Channel.

22 May: Prince Louis of France invades, landing at Sandwich in Kent.

June–August: Louis is admitted to the City of London; his forces also besiege Dover, Lincoln and Windsor, while Scottish forces re-enter England, besieging royal castles.

10 October: John falls ill with dysentery in Norfolk.

12 October: the king loses a large portion of his baggage train and treasure in the Wash.

18–19 October: John dies overnight at Newark, Nottinghamshire.

28 October: John's nine-year-old son is crowned Henry III at Gloucester, with royal government in the hands of William Marshal, Earl of Pembroke, and a council of thirteen.

12 November: Magna Carta is reissued by papal legate Guala Bicchieri and William Marshal in the name of Henry III; but war continues.

1217

20 May: The Battle of Lincoln against the rebellious barons ends in victory for William Marshal and the royal loyalists.

24 August: At sea, the Battle of Sandwich against the French ends in victory for Hubert de Burgh and the forces of the young Henry.

20 September: By the terms of the Treaty of Lambeth, France's Prince Louis agrees to leave England.

6 November: Magna Carta is reissued for a second time, now with the Charter of the Forest.

1225

Magna Carta and the Charter of the Forest are reissued in definitive versions in return for the grant of a tax on 'movables'.

1237

Magna Carta is reconfirmed by Henry III at a Westminster meeting described as a 'parliament'; it is to be enforced by sentence of excommunication against those who break it.

1253

Magna Carta is reissued, again in return for taxation, and again it is supported by the threat of excommunication.

1265

A Parliament called by rebel baron Simon de Montfort, Earl of Leicester, reissues Magna Carta and the Charter of the Forest, which are reconfirmed by Henry III.

1297

Edward I confirms Magna Carta and the Charter of the Forest, along with additional articles of reform, following political dispute with leading barons.

1300

The final confirmation of Magna Carta and the Charter of the Forest, by Edward I, takes place.

1508

Magna Carta appears in print for the first time, issued by Richard Pynson.

1619

Barrister and Parliamentarian Sir Edward Coke condemns royal abuses by the Stuart monarch James I, telling the House of Commons that they contravene Magna Carta.

1628

Sir Edward Coke's Petition of Right seeks to emulate Magna Carta in an attempt to bind James's successor, Charles I, to specific principles of government.

1687

Magna Carta is published in the American colonies.

1689

The Bill of Rights is passed by Parliament, as a statement of English law and customs.

1775

Massachusetts adopts as its symbol an American patriot holding a sword in one hand and Magna Carta in the other.

1791

An American Bill of Rights is ratified, designed to limit the powers of the newly independent country over its citizens.

1863

The Statute Law Revision Act strikes many clauses of Magna Carta from the British statute book.

1948

The new United Nations Organization produces its Universal Declaration of Human Rights, described by former US First Lady Eleanor Roosevelt as 'the international Magna Carta for all men everywhere'.

1957

The American Bar Association erects a permanent monument to Magna Carta at Runnymede.

1970

New British legislation strikes all but four clauses of Magna Carta from the statute book.

2007

A copy of Magna Carta 1297 is purchased at auction in New York City for $21.3 million.

2015

This year sees the 800th anniversary of Magna Carta.

The marble statue of James Madison, which stands in the James Madison Memorial Hall of the US Library of Congress. It was Madison, Fourth President of the United States, who deepened Magna Carta's influence on the evolving US Constitution through his amendments for the Bill of Rights in 1791.

JAMES MADISON
1751-1836

NOTES ON THE TEXT

INTRODUCTION

1   Ralph of Coggeshall, *Radulphi de Coggeshall Chronicon Anglicanum*, edited by J. Stevenson, Rolls Series No. 66 (1875), p. 170

2   'De principis instructione', in G. Warner (ed.), *Giraldus Cambrensis Opera*, (1891), p. 328

CHAPTER 1
ENGLAND REORDERED

1   Walter Map, *De Nugis Curialum*, edited and translated by M.R. James, revised by C.N.L. Brooke and R.A.B. Mynors (1983), p. 477

2   Ibid.

3   William of Newburgh, *The History of English Affairs*, edited and translated by P.G. Walsh and M.J. Kennedy, Book II (2007), p. 15

4   *Anglo-Saxon Chronicle*, edited by J.A. Giles (1914), p. 200

5   Thomas J. Keefe, 'King Henry II and the Earls: The Pipe Rolls Evidence', in *Albion*, Vol. 13, No. 3 (1981), Table 1, pp. 215–17

6   Barratt, Nick, 'Finance and the Economy in the Reign of Henry II', in C. Harper-Bill and N. Vincent (eds), *Henry II: New Perspectives* (2007), p. 249

7   R. Allen Brown, *English Castles*, new edition (2004), pp. 162–3

8   William of Newburgh, op. cit., Book I (1988)

9   H.M. Thomas, 'Shame, Masculinity and the Death of Thomas Becket', in *Speculum*, Vol. 87, No. 4 (2012), p. 1065

CHAPTER 2
WAR AND TAXES

1   Roger of Howden, *The Annals of Roger de Hoveden*, translated by Henry T. Riley (1853), Vol. II, p. 114

2   Ibid., p. 120

3   Barratt, Nick, 'The English Revenue of Richard I', in *English Historical Review,* Vol. 116, No. 467, p. 637. The 1188 Pipe Roll shows total income of £21,233, compared with £31,089 two years later, a rise of 47.6 per cent.

4   Roger of Howden, op. cit., pp. 290–1

5   Ibid., pp. 290–2

6   William Marshal's Life is a rich source of detail for this period: see A.J. Holden (ed.), D. Crouch and S. Gregory (trans.), *History of William Marshal*, 3 vols (2002–7), p. 18

7   Barratt, 'The English Revenue', op. cit., p. 637

CHAPTER 3
EMPIRE'S END

1   See John Gillingham, 'The Anonymous of Béthune, King John and Magna Carta', *passim*, in J.S. Loengard (ed.), *Magna Carta and the England of King John* (2010)

2   T. Wright, *The Political Songs of England* (1839), p. 6

3   R. Howlett (ed.), *Chronicles of the Reigns of Stephen, Henry II and Richard I*, Rolls Series No. 82, Vol. I (1884), p. 390

4   Gerald of Wales, *The Historical Works of Giraldus Cambrensis*, edited and revised by T. Wright (1894), p. 315

5   See J.C. Holt, *King John* (1963), p. 20

6   Gervase of Canterbury, *The Historical Works of Gervase of Canterbury*, edited by W. Stubbs, Vol. II (1880), pp. 92–3

CHAPTER 4
THE KING IN HIS KINGDOM

1   Analysed at length in T.K. Moore, 'The Loss of Normandy and the Invention of Terre Normannorum, 1204', in *English Historical Review*, Vol. 125, No. 516 (2010), pp. 1071–109

2   See Holt, op. cit., p. 13. When John visited York in 1200 he was the first English king to have been there for at least fourteen years. His visit to Newcastle the following year was the first since 1158.

3   J. Masschaele, 'The English Economy in the Age of Magna Carta', in Loengard, op. cit., p. 156. On prices, see P. Latimer, 'Early Thirteenth Century Prices' in S.D. Church (ed.), *King John: New Interpretations, passim* but especially pp. 69–73, Figs 1–9.

4   Masschaele, ibid., pp. 156–65

5   For John's annual revenue broken down by year, see Table 1 in Nick Barratt, 'The Revenue of King John', in *English Historical Review*, Vol. 111, No. 443 (1996), p. 839

CHAPTER 5
INTERDICT AND INTIMIDATION

1   Walter of Coventry, *Memoriale Fratris Walteri de Coventria*, edited by W. Stubbs (1872), Vol. II, p. 203

2   Barratt, 'The Revenue of King John', op. cit., p. 839

3   See S. Ambler, 'Feature of the Month: July 2014 – The Witness Lists to Magna Carta, 1215–1265', on the Magna Carta Project website: http://magnacarta.cmp.uea.ac.uk/read/feature_of_the_month/Jul_2014

4   King John's statement is printed and translated in Crouch, 'The Complaint of King John Against William de Briouze', in Loengard, op. cit., pp. 169–79

5   The Treaty of Falaise, such as it is known from later transcriptions, is printed in E.L.G. Stones (ed. and trans), *Anglo-Scottish Relations 1174–1328. Some Selected Documents* (1965), pp. 1–5. Richard's quitclaim of 1189 may be found here too, pp. 6–8.

6   The Treaty of Norham, ibid., pp. 12–13

7   J.C. Holt, *The Northerners: A Study in the Reign of King John* (1961), p. 79

CHAPTER 6
CRISIS AND MACHINATIONS

1   Holt, *Magna Carta*, op. cit., pp. 190–1

CHAPTER 7
A MEADOW CALLED RUNNYMEDE

1. The original Unknown Charter is held in the French Archives Nationales, Archives du Royaume J.655. It is printed, and its dating discussed, in Holt, *Magna Carta*, op. cit., Appendix 4, pp. 418–28. The Unknown Charter may be found translated into English in *English Historical Documents*, Vol. III (1975), edited by H. Rothwell, pp. 310–11.

2   For a recent analysis of Langton's role in the negotiations of May–June 1215, see D. Carpenter, 'Archbishop Langton and Magna Carta: His Contribution, His Doubts and His Hypocrisy', in *English Historical Review*, 126, No. 522 (2011), pp. 1041–65.

3   The historiographical arguments are summed up, and a very sensible timetable offered, in D. Carpenter, 'The Dating and Making of Magna Carta', in his *The Reign of Henry III* (1996), pp. 1–16. The present account leans heavily on the sequence of events suggested there.

4   To be found, with discussion, in Holt, *Magna Carta*, op. cit., Appendix 5, pp. 429–40, and in English translation in *English Historical Documents*, Vol. III, op. cit., pp. 311–16.

CHAPTER 8
A CHARTER OF LIBERTIES

1   Holt, *Magna Carta*, op. cit., p. 255

2   Recent editions of the text of Magna Carta can be found in *English Historical Documents*, Vol. III, op. cit., pp. 316–24, where it is translated into English, and in Holt, *Magna Carta*, op. cit., pp. 441–73, where it is in facing-page translation, with a short introductory discussion of the differences between the four surviving editions of the charter.

3   See Carpenter, 'Archbishop Langton', op. cit.

4   *Ego respectu dei et amore quem erga uos [omnes] habeo, sanctam dei ecclesiam in primis liberam facio* ('Out of respect for God and the love I have towards you [all], in the first place I cause God's church to be free); see www.earlyenglishlaws.ac.uk/laws/texts/hn-cor/view

5   On this aspect of John of Salisbury's thought, see N.M. Fryde, 'The Roots of Magna Carta: Opposition to the Plantagenets', in J. Canning and O.G. Oexle (eds), *Political Thought and the Realities of Power in the Middle Ages* (1998), pp. 59–60 and Note 37.

CHAPTER 9
WAR AND INVASION

1   Pope Innocent's letter is printed in translation in *English Historical Documents*, Vol. III, op. cit., pp. 324–6.

2   *History of William Marshal*, op. cit.

3   Walter of Coventry, op. cit., p. 228

CHAPTER 10
AFTERLIFE OF THE CHARTER

1   *History of William Marshal*, op. cit.

2   Roger of Wendover, op. cit., p. 205

3   The 1225 edition of Magna Carta and the Charter of the Forest are printed in Holt, *Magna Carta*, op. cit., Appendices 12 and 13, pp. 501–17, and translated in *English Historical Documents*, Vol. III, op. cit., pp. 341–9.

4   D. Carpenter, 'Feature of the Month: April 2014', on the Magna Carta Project website: http://magnacartaresearch. org/read/feature_of_the_month/Apr_2014

5   The account of this episode by Matthew Paris may be found in H.R. Luard (ed.) *Matthaei Parisiensis, Monachi Sancti Albani Chronica Majora*, Vol. IV (1877), pp. 185–7.

6   S. Ambler, 'Feature of the Month: March 2014 – Henry III's Confirmation of Magna Carta in March 1265', on the Magna Carta Project website: http://magnacarta.cmp.uea. ac.uk/read/feature_of_the_month/Mar_2014

7   R. Horrox (ed.), *Parliament Rolls of Medieval England*, Vol. XVI (2012), January 1497: Item 9

8   Held in the British Library: BL C.112.a.2.

9   Coke, quoted in F. Thompson, *Magna Carta: Its Role in the Making of the English Constitution 1300–1629* (1948), p. 302

10   A. Cromartie, 'The Constitutionalist Revolution: The Transformation of Political Culture in Early Stuart England', in *Past & Present*, No. 163 (May 1999), p. 101

11   R.V. Turner, 'The Meaning of Magna Carta Since 1215', in *History Today*, Vol. 53, No. 9 (2003); online at: www.historytoday.com/ralph-v-turner/meaning-magna-carta-1215

12   The full text of Mandela's speech may be found on the ANC website: www.anc.org.za/show.php?id=3430.

13   D. Cameron, 'British values aren't optional, they're vital. That's why I will promote them in EVERY school', in the *Daily Mail* (15 June 2014).

14   See, for example, the interview with web pioneer Tim Berners-Lee: J. Kiss, 'An Online Magna Carta: Berners-Lee Calls for Bill of Rights for Web', in *The Guardian* (12 March 2014)

15   A. Rickell, 'A New Magna Carta', *disabilitynow* (2009): www.disabilitynow.org.uk/article/new-magna-carta; T. Kahle, 'Miners for Democracy and the Planet', in *Socialist Worker* (24 June 2014): http://socialistworker.org/ 2014/06/24/miners-fighting-for-the-planet; J. Casillas, 'Magna Carta for Medical Banking': www.himss.org/files/ HIMSSorg/content/files/medicalBankingProject/MBP_ Magna_Carta_Aligning_Banks_Healthcare.pdf; J. Galolo, 'BPOs, workers back proposal to exempt OT, graveyard pay from taxes', *Sun Star Cebu* (7 July 2014): www.sunstar. com.ph/cebu/business/2014/07/07/bpos-workers-back-proposal-exempt-ot-graveyard-pay-taxes-352400.

APPENDIX III
THE ENFORCERS OF MAGNA CARTA

1   Luard, op. cit., Vol. II, p. 605

2   Lambeth Palace Library MS 371 fo. 56v, reprinted in Holt, *Magna Carta*, op. cit., Appendix 8, pp.479–80

FURTHER READING

The following is a concise list of secondary books and articles. Leading primary sources are mentioned in the Notes.

Barratt, Nick, 'The English Revenue of Richard I', in *English Historical Review*, Vol. 116, No. 467 (2001), pp. 635–56

Breay, Claire, *Magna Carta: Manuscripts and Myths* (2010)

Brown, R.Allen, *English Castles*, revised edition (2004)

Carpenter, D.A., *The Reign of Henry III* (1996)
——, 'Archbishop Langton and Magna Carta: His Contribution, His Doubts and His Hypocrisy', in *English Historical Review*, Vol. 126, No. 522 (2011), pp. 1041–65

Church, S.D. (ed.), *King John: New Interpretations* (1999)

Cromartie, A., 'The Constitutionalist Revolution: The Transformation of Political Culture in Early Stuart England', in *Past & Present*, No. 163 (May 1999), pp. 76–120

Fryde, Natalie, 'The Roots of Magna Carta: Opposition to the Plantagenets', in J. Canning and O. Oexle (eds), *Political Thought and the Realities of Power in the Middle Ages* (1998)

Holt, J.C., *The Northerners: A Study in the Reign of King John* (1961)
——, *King John* (1963)
——, *Magna Carta*, 2nd edition (1992)

Jolliffe, J.E.A., *Angevin Kingship*, 2nd edition (1963)

Keefe, Thomas K., 'King Henry II and the Earls: The Pipe Roll Evidence', in *Albion*, Vol. 13, No. 3 (1981), pp 191–222

Loengard, J.S. (ed.), *Magna Carta and the England of King John* (2010)

McGlynn, S., *Blood Cries Afar: The Forgotten Invasion of England, 1216* (2011)

McKechnie, W.S., *Magna Carta*, 2nd edition (1914)

Magna Carta Project:
http://magnacarta.cmp.uea.ac.uk

Moore, Tony, 'The Loss of Normandy and the Invention of Terre Normannorum, 1204', in *English Historical Review*, Vol. 125, No. 516 (2010), pp. 1071–109

Sandoz, E., *The Roots of Liberty: Magna Carta, Ancient Constitution and the Anglo-American Tradition of the Rule of Law*, new edition (2008)

Thomas, Hugh M., 'Shame, Masculinity and the Death of Thomas Becket', in *Speculum*, Vol. 87, No. 4 (2012), pp. 1050–88

Thompson, Faith, *Magna Carta: Its Role in the Making of the English Constitution 1300–1629* (1948)

Turner, R.V., 'The Meaning of Magna Carta Since 1215', in *History Today*, Vol. 53, No. 9 (2003): online at www.historytoday.com

Vincent, Nicholas, *Magna Carta: A Very Short Introduction* (2012)

Warren, W.L., *Henry II* (1973)

INDEX

PICTURE CREDITS

Page: 13 British Library Cotton
Claudius D. II, f. 73; 18 SSPL / Getty
Images; 24–5 British Museum / Art
Archive; 28 Manuel Cohen / Art
Archive; 34 British Library Royal 14
C. VII, f. 9; 38 39 DeA Picture
Library / Art Archive; 42, 45 British
Library MS Royal 14.C VII, f. 5v /
Topfoto; 46 Neil Holmes/
Bridgeman Images; 51 DeA Picture
Library / G. Nimatallah/ Art
Archive; 54 Library of Congress;
62–3 British Museum / Ealdgyth
Wikimedia Commons;
65 Bibliothèque Municipale
Castres / Gianni Dagli Orti / Art
Archive; 70 Jarrold Publishing /
Art Archive; 76 British Library
Additional MS 4838 / Art
Archive; 83 Granger Collection /
Topfoto; 86–7 British Library
Cotton MS Augustus ii. 106 /
Wikipedia; 90 British Library / Art
Archive; 94 MS 16, f. 50v (detail)
Parker Library / Corpus Christi
College Cambridge; 97 Topfoto;
102 NotFromUtrecht / Wikimedia
Commons; 109 Corporation of
London /HIP/ Tofoto; 113 Library
of Congress; 123 JJ Harrison /
Wikimedia Commons; 128 The
National Archives and Records
Administration; 137 Alex Wong /
Getty Images; 152–3 Temple
Church, London / Bridgeman
Images; 157 British Library Royal 14
C. VII, f. 119 /AKG; 163 The Print
Collector/ Getty Images; 170 British
Library Cotton Vitellius A.XIII,
f.6; 173 MS 16, f. 55v (detail) Parker
Library / Corpus Christi College
Cambridge; 177 British Library
Royal 16 G VI f. 362v; 183 Library
of Congress.

ACKNOWLEDGEMENTS

The first essay I ever wrote about England's medieval history was on the subject of King John and Magna Carta, and it has been both enjoyable and refreshing to return to the subject exactly a decade and a half later. My supervisor at Cambridge in 1999 was Dr Helen Castor – and Helen was kind enough to revisit old ground by reading the manuscript of this book. Now, as then, she offered many perceptive comments on my work. I am incredibly lucky to call her a colleague and a friend.

The staff at The National Archives, The British Library, the London Library, Lincoln Cathedral and Salisbury Cathedral were all very helpful while I wrote this book. Professor Louise Wilkinson of Canterbury Christ Church University generously offered her thoughts on this book during its writing as did Dr Suzannah Lipscomb of New College of the Humanities. Julian Harrison at The British Library was kind enough to set me in the right direction in thinking about Magna Carta's international legacy. Dr Nick Barratt at The National Archives gave me his advice on several matters of early Plantagenet history. Conversations with Professor David Carpenter of King's College, London, and Dr Julie Barrau of Emmanuel College, Cambridge, changed the way I thought about particular aspects of this story. Marta Musso helped with several elements of the research. It should be obvious that none of these brilliant people are responsible for any errors of fact or judgement to be found here.

I am grateful to everyone at Head of Zeus, especially to Anthony Cheetham for suggesting in the first place that this book might be written. Richard Milbank and Mark Hawkins-Dady brought the manuscript to publication with exceptional diligence and skill.

Special thanks, as ever, to Walter Donohue, to my peerless agent, Georgina Capel, and to my girls: Jo, Violet and Ivy Jones. All of them, in their different ways, keep me going.

Dan Jones, October 2014